I PROMISE IT WON'T ALWAYS HURT LIKE THIS

18 ASSURANCES *on* GRIEF

CLARE MACKINTOSH

 sourcebooks

Published by Sourcebooks
P.O. Box 4410, Naperville, Illinois 60567-4410
(630) 961-3900
sourcebooks.com

Originally published as *I Promise It Won't Always Hurt Like This* in 2024
in Great Britain by Sphere, an imprint of Little Brown Book Group.
This edition issued based on the hardcover edition published in 2024 in
Great Britain by Sphere, an imprint of Little Brown Book Group.

Cataloging-in-Publication Data is on file with the Library of Congress.

Printed and bound in the United States of America.
POD

For everyone who has ever loved, then lost.
And for Alex.

Introduction

I am in my forties. I have lost grandparents, a father, a child. Grief has run through my life like thread through fabric; at times gossamer-thin and barely there, other times weaving thick, clumsy darns across the rips. In my grief, I am a mother, a child, a sister, a wife, a woman, a friend.

I am also a writer. I have touched on grief in everything I have written, because grief has touched every part of me. I write to make sense of the world, and of my place in it, and I write to find people who feel the same way I do. I write in the hope that my words will resonate with others; that they will read a line over and over and say, *This. This is how I feel.*

My novels circle around the subject of loss, yet I have never written explicitly about grief. About how it feels, about the shape of it, the awfulness of it. About its changing nature, its patterns and passing.

I have never written about *my* grief.

It has always felt too big to tackle without the filter of fiction; too dangerous—like looking directly at the sun. What if it blinds me? What if, once my eyes are locked on it, I can't look away? For a long time, I managed my grief by compartmentalizing it. It is a skill honed during my years as a police officer, when carrying the emotional baggage from one job to another would be damaging to all concerned. I parceled out my emotions into neat bundles and locked them away until I had the space and strength to unpack them.

I have not always unpacked them.

Some moments—some feelings—are so hard and so heavy they stay in their boxes, like the nostalgia we cart around from new house to new house, filling our attics and garages and under-stairs closet. Relics of another time; baggage we no longer need. We have not touched it for years, yet we can't quite sever ourselves from it. It is a part of us.

If I wrote about my grief, I thought, I would have to unpack the boxes. I would have to take out my feelings and examine them, one by one. It could break me. It *would* break me. And so I continued to touch on the subject lightly, through my characters, like a child who pushes someone bigger and braver in front of them.

Yet here we are: at the start of a book that is very much about grief. You and me, staring at the sun.

As it turned out, the catalyst for writing wasn't grief itself but the absence of it. Four years ago, halfway through the fourteenth anniversary of my son's death, I realized what day it was. I had known the date, but the significance had slipped into the recesses of my mind, the way it does when you've promised to be somewhere or to do something but can't remember where or what.

The penny dropped at the garden center, midway through the serious business of choosing the perfect Christmas tree. The scent of pine needles was heady and comforting, and I stood for a moment in this temporary indoor forest. I surveyed my emotions, as though I were a first-aider at the scene of an accident, running my fingers gently from one side of the patient to the other, checking for fractures. How did I feel? How serious were my injuries? Was I still breathing?

I was.

———

My son Alex was five weeks old when he died.

I find myself unable to give you a simple cause of death. The tipping point for an elderly man with terminal cancer might be organ collapse, or malnutrition, yet we'd still blame cancer for taking him. A young woman killed in a car accident might have had a fatal head injury, yet the cause of her death is surely the crash. My son was born at twenty-eight weeks, and—if not exactly hale and hearty—his prognosis was good. Better, in fact, than that of his twin brother, who went straight onto a ventilator, machinery keeping him alive where I had failed. Both boys exceeded expectations, gaining weight and feeding well, avoiding the myriad health problems associated with prematurity.

Consequently, Alex's rapid descent at three weeks old was unexpected and terrifying. Tests revealed the presence of pseudomonas—a bacteria that falls under the benign-sounding umbrella "hospital bug," as though it's something one can easily shake off. And perhaps he could have done had he not been premature, had he not weighed barely three pounds, had he not, then, developed meningitis.

Did he die from meningitis?

From the subsequent brain hemorrhage?

Or from the decision my husband and I ultimately made to bring an end to his suffering?

Death, like life, is rarely straightforward.

———

In the days following Alex's death, I was continually surprised to find myself still alive. It seemed impossible that my body could continue to function when I was experiencing what felt like multiple organ failure. My extremities were numb and tingling, as though my blood had taken one look at the distance required to travel there and decided against it. Something crushed my chest: my ribs were surely broken, my lungs a fraction of their usual size. My breath came shallow and jagged, each inhalation briefer than the one before, each exhalation harder than the last. A dark cloud seeped into my brain, like ink through a blotter, fogging my thoughts and weighing down my limbs.

In short, I was dying.

And yet I did not die, and there were times when that felt like a second cruelty.

———

Over the years, my grief has changed shape, its jagged edges softening to something easier to carry. It has altered its behavior, becoming less demanding, less needy. Without exception, these transitions have happened while I've been looking the other way, the way a train journey swallows the kilometers when you're absorbed in a book. I looked up on that fourteenth anniversary, surrounded by Christmas trees, and realized I had traveled further than I'd thought possible. I hadn't woken that morning with heartache so overwhelming I couldn't speak, as I had every year before. There was no longer something pressing on my chest, making every breath feel like my last. My grief was still present, but it no longer consumed me.

It has gotten easier.

It will get easier for you, too.

That's my promise. It's a small thing to write a whole book about, isn't it? But I've found that listening to something once isn't enough to believe it, especially when your head is telling you something else entirely.

It was your fault.

You should have done more.

If only,

If only,

If only...

More—much more—on that later.

There is nothing magic about fourteen years. If you're suffering with loss right now, that feeling is real and raw. It could be three years, or seven, or twenty, before you wake without grief lodged in your throat. I know how much it hurts. But I know, too, as intimately and surely as I know grief itself, that you will not always feel this way.

We can try to analyze grief. We can herd our emotions into clearly labeled stages. We can discuss the science behind the physical pain we're feeling. But grief is bigger than that, more willful. It follows its own path. Over the years, I've learned not to fight my grief but to be mindful of it. To accept it as part of me, just as I accept the creaks and scars, the gray hairs and the lines.

———

This book is structured around a series of promises: my commitment to you that the sun will rise again. It is a conversation, not a lecture; a story of hope, not of loss. It's a book to return to when you're hurting; to give to a friend when you don't know what to say. A book to pick up when you need a gentle voice to keep you company. There are eighteen promises, one for each year I have now lived without my son; each year I have grown around my grief.

Few people talk openly about death, and I remember feeling so lonely in my early grief. I didn't know if I was "doing it right"—if what I was feeling was normal—and I didn't know where to find the answers.

The short answer is that whatever you're feeling is normal.

The longer answer is this book.

On 10 December 2020—the fourteenth anniversary of Alex's death—after we'd chosen a Christmas tree and driven home, I shared my thoughts online. I wanted to offer hope to anyone still at the start of their journey through grief, to reassure them that it wouldn't always hurt so much. I wanted, too, to mark the moment for myself. It felt like a milestone. An achievement, even—because grieving is an active act, not a passive one.

Four years later, I still receive messages every day in response to that post. I have read tens of thousands of stories, from people all over the world, in different phases of grief. I have cried for those who see no way forward and been gladdened by those who are not only surviving but thriving. I replied to as many messages as I could, and when I couldn't keep up, I wrote this book. For a while, the words I'd posted on Twitter were enough. They had reached almost twenty million people, and I knew from the responses that they'd provided comfort.

But there was more I wanted to say.

I wanted to add to the promises I'd made and supply practical suggestions to accompany them. I realized I was finally ready to unpack my own grief and consider which elements were universal. My son would have turned eighteen this year, and it feels right to be working on something in his name; a coming-of-age for my grief instead of for my boy.

I am thinking, too, how hard I found it to be online when my grief was at its peak; that a poorly worded comment or a misplaced advert could derail me for days.

But a book…

A book contains only what it promises on the cover. There's nothing sliding into your private messages or jumping into your timeline. A book hands the power back to the reader.

And so this is my journey through grief, but it's yours, too. In every corner of the world, every minute of every day, people are mourning loved ones. Grief is universal. But just as our experiences of death are different, so, too, are the emotions that follow. Your grief is as unique as you are—as unique as your relationship was with the person you've lost—and whatever you are feeling is valid and true. I have focused on the elements of grief that seem to be common to so many of us, based on the messages I received. There will be pages you will want to read over and over, in which you'll place bookmarks or pieces of torn paper or make handwritten notes in the margin. *This. This is how I feel.* But there will also be chapters where the words don't speak to you in the same way—where you feel as though they're talking to someone else entirely—and that's okay, too. Skip over those pages, and don't for a second worry that you're doing something wrong by not feeling the same way I did. We all grieve in our own way.

I am not a bereavement expert. I am no different to you, except that—perhaps—I am a little further along this journey neither of us wanted to take. I couldn't have written this book when I was first bereaved, but I wish I could have read it. I wish I'd had something to reach for at the precise moment I needed it.

Over the years, I have read many books on grief—and tried to read many more. Soon after I was bereaved, at the time I most needed to find solace in a book, I found instead overwhelming lists of things I should be doing. I found impenetrable psychology in dense paragraphs that tried to explain why I was feeling the way I was when the reason was really quite simple. My son had died. It didn't help me—not then—to understand how cortisol was flooding my brain, or how my prefrontal cortex (the part responsible for decision-making) had temporarily retired. What I wanted to know was that it would get better. That I wasn't alone.

Your friends and family will reach out to you on special days—Christmas, anniversaries, due dates—but even the closest of friends can't always predict the triggers that take even you by surprise. A chord in a song you heard on the last holiday you took together; the drift of a perfume you once found on your pillow every day. The swish of someone's hair; a glimpse of a scarf in a shop window. A pair of shoes, a photograph, a wine label. Daffodils.

This book is for those moments.

You may find, as I did, that it is impossible to concentrate for any great length of time and, for this reason, there is no overarching narrative in this book—no obligation to plow through a hundred pages of dark times before hope emerges. You can read the book in the conventional way, from start to finish, or you can draw courage from a single chapter. When even that feels overwhelming, the list of promises on their own might bring you comfort.

However you read it, I hope it helps. I promise you—and I will keep promising until you believe me—it won't always hurt like this.

Promises

1. I promise it won't always hurt like this,
2. that you won't always lie awake at night, sobbing until you cannot breathe.
3. I promise the waves of grief that knock you off your feet won't drown you.
4. I promise you will find a way to say goodbye,
5. and a reason to keep going.
6. I promise this won't always be your first thought in the morning,
7. that you won't always fear the worst.
8. I promise you won't always feel so angry,
9. so guilty,
10. so tired.
11. I promise you'll find someone who understands.
12. I promise that you won't always be winded by someone else's happiness,
13. broken by anniversaries
14. or by questions you cannot answer.
15. I promise you will be happy again,
16. that one day you'll be able to pay it forward.
17. I promise you won't forget.
18. I promise it won't always hurt like this.

1

I promise it won't always hurt like this

I couldn't tell you what month it was, but there were daffodils, so it must have been spring. A few weeks after Alex died, I suppose. Two months at most. The heads of the daffodils were heavy with rain, their stems wrapped in damp paper towels and aluminum foil. Attached to the flowers was a woman.

"How are you?" she asked.

How was I?

I was dying. My heartbeat was erratic, a pulse thrumming in my ears like an overhead jet. My skin hurt as though I had the flu, so sensitive to touch I could only wear the softest clothes—clothes that hadn't seen the inside of a washing machine for a week or more. My husband was at work and our surviving twin still in intensive care, so the woman must have caught me in a rare moment at home. I wondered if she'd called by at other times, if the daffodils were on their second or third outing.

"I'm okay," I said. Because that's the script, isn't it? I imagine you've said it, too, standing upright, shoulders back and chin raised to hide the fact that, inside, you're disappearing. Or would like to. You tilt your head to match theirs.

"I doubt that," said the daffodil woman. "May I come in?"

I shuffled aside. The woman was a stranger, but that in itself had ceased to be strange. The weeks had been full of uninvited guests: doctors, funeral directors, bereavement counselors. Once, a priest, sent at the request of a family friend in another town. I didn't ask for any of them. I didn't want any of them. None of us does, yet grief brings them all to our door.

Our house at the time was tall and thin. There was a tiny walled garden at the front, where the cat slept in a flower bed and the gate banged in the wind when the postman left it open. I was the local police sergeant, and my commute to work was from one end of the high street to the other, clipping on my tie as I finished my breakfast toast. I hadn't been at work for a long time, and I couldn't foresee a time when I would go back.

"I'm so sorry your son died," the woman said when we were sitting down. I might have offered her a cup of tea; she might have accepted. I was staring at the daffodils, at the tiny fruit flies crawling out of them, but at the sound of her words I looked up.

Whoever this woman was, she'd lost someone, too.

You can tell, don't you think? Sometimes it's in the way people hold themselves, the direct smile that doesn't slide away in the way so many well-meaning gazes do, as though it hurts to see our pain. But mostly it's the way they speak. Statements of fact instead of euphemisms. Direct. Almost blunt. This is what's happened. It's awful, but there it is. Unavoidable. Someone died.

"What was his name?" she asked.

I believe this to be the single most important question you can ask someone grieving, yet I can count on one hand the number of people who have asked it. They ask, instead, *How did he die?*, as though the cause were more important than the life it took.

My son's name was Alex. We chose Alexander, knowing it was too big a name for such a small boy. When he was born, I placed my little finger into the curl of his hand and imagined the man he would one day become.

So much of grief is about absence, isn't it? Not only the absence of the one we love, but the stealing of memories not yet created. The opportunities missed. The father who doesn't get to walk his daughter down the aisle; the grandmother who misses out on holding her first grandchild. Alex, who never grew into his name.

I wish I could remember the daffodil woman's name. I wish I remembered the name of the child she'd lost. She stayed for an hour or so, and all the time I clutched the flowers she'd brought and stared at those tiny flies. She had picked them from her garden, I suppose. Taken the time to collect them, wrap them in damp paper, and bring them to the door of a stranger who couldn't even make eye contact. It remains one of the kindest things anyone has ever done for me.

"I promise it won't always hurt like this," the woman said. Her own grief had been unbearable, she said, in the beginning. She had thought she would die from the pain. She had been unable to speak, to move, to function. She told me about her son, and about how he'd died all those years ago. I listened to her voice, matter-of-fact and calm, and for a million pounds I would never have shared the thought in my head as she spoke.

I'll tell you, though.

I thought: *You can't have really loved him.*

I'm not proud of it, but grief isn't all soft-focus walks through graveyards and quiet sobbing over kitchen tables. Grief isn't romantic; it's painful and ugly, as often filled with anger and bitterness as love. Unless someone tells you the terrible thoughts they've had, you will imagine you're the only one, and grief is lonely enough without that. Beneath every promise in this book is one underlying principle: I promise to be honest with you.

If the daffodil woman had truly loved her son, I reasoned, she wouldn't be able to talk about him so easily. *Look at you,* I thought, *properly dressed, with a job, a family, a life. I will never be like that again. My son has died, and I will never, ever get over it.*

"It's very early days for you," the woman said. "But I promise it will get easier."

———

Afterward, I stood in the kitchen and cried until I couldn't breathe. I had meant to put the daffodils in water, but finding a vase was beyond my capabilities, and instead they wilted on the drainboard. I didn't care. I didn't want daffodils. I might, I decided, never want daffodils again.

Things would not *get easier*.

Whatever grief my unexpected visitor had endured was nothing compared to mine. My own grief was real. It was raw and agonizing and it was going to destroy me. In years to come, I would not speak about my son with composure, I would not turn up at a stranger's door with daffodils and comfort, because I would still be broken myself.

My grief was different.

———

As I write this, it is February. Still winter, technically, but there are signs of spring everywhere I look, and morning frosts give way to blue skies on enough days to hint at better times ahead. Our new house has a garden—a long, wide lawn that stretches toward fields—and poking through the grass beneath the trees are dozens of daffodils, waiting to flower. Every autumn, I plant dozens more, burying them beneath the peeled-back turf like treasure. The thought of them carries me through the winter. I can't see them, but I know they are there: promises of spring, riding out the dark days until it is time.

In the supermarket, buckets of daffodils sit by the cash registers, rubber-banded and quiet in bud. They cost a pound each. A pound! Where else can you buy hope for a pound? I take a bunch every week, dripping water over my shopping. The flowers open two days later, sunny and smiling, and every time I see them, I think of my boy.

I prefer to leave my garden daffs in the ground—it seems unfair to uproot them when they've worked so hard to flower where they stand—but sometimes I snip a few long stems for a vase.

"What's that weird smell?" asks a teenager, drifting into

my study. That same teenager who all those years ago was still in intensive care. That same teenager who lost a twin brother the day I lost a child.

"It's spring," I say, but he's already gone in search of something more interesting than his mother and a vase of lopsided flowers. My fingers hover over my keyboard. I've lost my thread. A tiny insect climbs out from the trumpet of a daffodil before picking its way around its frilly edges, each undulation a miniature mountain to climb.

It will get easier, the woman said. Not better, but easier.

And it has.

2

I promise you won't always lie awake at night, sobbing until you cannot breathe

When Alex became critically, catastrophically ill, we were taken away from the ward to a room known as the Quiet Room. It was at the end of a corridor, and as we followed the consultant, I felt like Alice, tumbled down a rabbit hole into a world in which I didn't belong. The corridor stretched long, and I wanted it to stretch longer so I never reached the end. But there we were. Our son's disabilities, the consultant said, would be global. It was possible that he would never breathe independently; even if he did, he would never walk, or talk, or swallow. It was doubtful he would have any awareness of the world around him.

How I hated that room, filled with the echoes of bad news; with the tears of countless parents who dreaded the future and wept for the past. I started crying the moment the doctor began talking, and I thought I would never stop.

"It's time to make a decision," they said. Someone pushed a fresh box of tissues toward me, and I stared at it, letting my tears fall, fat and ugly. I watched the knees of my jeans darken with salt water. For five weeks, doctors had made all the decisions. We had listened helplessly as drugs and fluids were stopped and started; watched as nurses moved in swiftly to silence an alarm with increased oxygen. Yet now, at this most critical of times, the decision was ours?

You know the path we chose. Had we chosen otherwise, this would be a different book.

There was a baptism. The hospital chaplain, sandwiched between Perspex cribs; holy water, administered from a bottle; Alex in a white gown borrowed from the hospital. I wondered how many other babies had worn it, and how long they had lived afterward.

In the car on the way home from the hospital, I couldn't stop crying. My son wasn't dead, but tomorrow he would be. Twenty-four hours has never felt so long or gone so fast.

———

You may have been bereaved suddenly, or you may—like me—have had advance notice of the inevitable. A terminal diagnosis, a period of illness. An impossible decision. This anticipatory grief is no less painful than that after the event, and in many ways it is harder to cope with. You may feel the need to "put on a brave face" for the person who is dying, or to stay strong to do the numerous practical things required of a carer. However conclusive the situation, there remains the desperate hope that something might change—a second opinion, a new medication, a miracle—and this blind faith can in itself be exhausting.

As we drew closer to home, my husband slowed the car. There was a deer in the road, on the edge of Blenheim Palace estate. She was too badly hurt to live, but fighting hard to try; limbs flailing, lungs heaving. Driving away seemed impossible; hastening her departure equally so. We got out of the car and sat with her in the moonlight, waiting till she was quiet and still. We took shuddering lungfuls of cold air, unable to find words for the nightmare in which we'd found ourselves, bracing ourselves for what was to come.

Alex's life-support machine was switched off the next day. They brought him to the Quiet Room, where the tissues were still untouched. I felt a sudden, unjust flash of anger that no other parent had been given such terrible news in the last twenty-four hours. The doctor left Alex with us, and for the first time—and the last—it was just the three of us.

Outside, I could hear a phone ringing, the nurses going about their business. Someone was laughing. My world stopped turning.

———

Afterward, we didn't want to go home. We were afraid of being alone, I think, and we felt—suddenly—more like children than parents. We drove to my family home, and as our headlights lit up the drive, the front door opened and my mother stood there, her face ashen. I remembered standing where she was and opening that same door some twenty years earlier, the day my grandfather died. I was shaken, in the way young people are when they see grown-ups cry; when they realize adults have the same feelings they do. My father had seemed cross, and it was only much later, when I was an adult myself, that I understood how easily sorrow and anger trade places.

"I'm going to need you all more than ever," my grandmother said as we stood in that open doorway. She was tiny; birdlike and frail. I had wondered then how someone could age so much in a single day. Now I understood. As my husband and I walked toward the house, I buckled under the weight of my grief.

My mother held out her arms. "Oh, my baby." She was trying not to cry, but faced with my stricken tears, she gave in to her own.

———

The grief of the people who love you is twofold. Their hearts break once at the death of a grandchild, a friend, a sibling; they break a second time when they see your pain.

———

In those early days, it felt as though I did nothing but cry. Only *"crying"* was too passive a word for what I was experiencing. Sobs heaved from somewhere deep inside me; earthquakes breaking through the surface with molten tears that burned my skin and never seemed to stop. My stomach ached, my throat was sore, and my face was raw, yet still I sobbed.

My husband cried, too. His own grief is not mine to share, but I think he will permit me to stray a little out of my lane on this one point. I do not believe that men and women grieve differently, but despite all the advances in equality we have made in the last few decades, we continue to expect men to be stronger than women. It is a dangerous, damaging presumption that hinders, rather than helps, our recovery from grief.

"How's she doing?" I heard one evening, in a low voice at the front door. A neighbor, calling with a lasagna for the freezer. She must have been looking out for our car; we had barely taken off our coats after ten hours at the hospital. I was standing in the kitchen, a dish towel useless in my hands. I didn't go to the door. I appreciated the kindness—I *needed* it—but so often back then, I couldn't take it. Instead, I looked at the layer of grease on the untouched cooker. I unfolded the dish towel and folded it another way.

"We're getting there," I heard my husband say. I wondered

where "there" was. I couldn't visualize an end to the way we were living; to the exhaustion of the constant tears, the lack of sleep.

"Let us know if there's anything we can do. And look after her, yes?"

Look after her.

No one ever told me to *look after* my husband back then. I tried to imagine what that pressure felt like: to stumble under the weight of your own grief, then be burdened with the responsibility for someone else's. For so few people to ask after your own recovery that you fall silent on the subject. The maxim that "big boys don't cry" is—I think—slowly disappearing, but its legacy remains. If we value our mental health, we need to move past gender expectations and give men the same freedom as women to grieve and cry.

———

There is a reason why some people actively seek out weepy films; why we sometimes say, "I probably just need a good cry." Crying *is* good. Emotional tears release chemicals (oxytocin and endogenous opioids) that reduce stress and pain. Oxytocin is the same "happy hormone" released during childbirth, breastfeeding, massage, social contact, and sexual intimacy—it's our body's way of making us feel better.

In the weeks after Alex died, I did not feel as though I were being flooded with happy hormones. I lurched from one fit of sobbing to another, filling the intermission with silent tears. With no time to recover between bouts, my head was permanently thick, pounding with the effort of keening. It *was* doing me good—I just didn't have the space to feel it.

Things are different now.

This book has made me cry. It was inevitable, and because of that, I have been careful about when and where I have written it. When I'm writing a novel, I often take my laptop to a café or bar, drawing inspiration from the world around me. Not so for this book. For this book, I have shut myself in my office. I have drawn the curtains and put a note on the door, and watched the clock so as to leave myself time to recover. Nowadays, the tears come with a warning. I feel a pressure build in my chest, like water pushing against a dam, like a rising tide. I feel it in my throat—a hard lump I can't swallow.

What I have now, that I didn't have then, is a choice.

I can cry—and feel the subsequent release—or I can say no. Get up from my desk, go for a walk. Open the curtains, take a shower, switch to writing something else. Slowly, that lump in my throat will soften, and the pressure in my chest will ease.

In those early stages of grief, we can't walk away. It clings to us. It *is* us.

You might feel—as you drag yourself through another night of despair, as you walk across a carpet littered with spent tissues—that life will always be this way. You might sob until you pass out, until you cannot breathe because your nose is blocked and your head is pounding and your eyes are swollen closed, and you might think that you will never be free of these tears.

But you will, I promise.

———

Four years after Alex died, my father died, too.

It will be okay, I thought. *I know what grief is like. I know what to do.*

It wasn't okay.

Grief isn't like buying a car, or changing jobs; we don't handle it better the more we experience it. Grief is different every time, and as another loss stacks against the last, it can feel as though we're living each one over again.

I was in a police training course when my mother called, my phone vibrating in the pocket of my uniform. I knew, before I answered, what she would say.

"He's gone."

Perhaps it was down to the uniform that I hardly faltered, that I gathered my things, spoke quietly to the course leader, and drove to the hospice at Stoke Mandeville hospital. I felt completely numb, focused on the practicalities; on finding the room, supporting my mother. I was holding it together the same way I handled a crisis at work; objective and unemotional—so very different to the immediate aftermath of Alex's death.

I walked into my father's room to find my mother by the bed, crying. Behind her, French doors opened onto a courtyard garden, calm and beautiful, with willowy trees dappling the sun. I had a sudden memory of the day Alex had died, of my mother in the doorway of my childhood home, and I felt as though the world had tilted. I felt the familiar lump in my throat—the pressure in my chest—and I wanted to cry, but nothing happened.

Nothing happened for weeks. Not afterward, when my sisters arrived, or at the funeral, when I stood on shaky legs to read a eulogy for a man I adored.

I thought I knew grief. Grief was physical pain, it was endless sobbing, it was wanting to die. I didn't understand why I felt so different when my love was no less. This grief was unrecognizable. It was numbness, coating my senses till I couldn't feel anything, till I felt as though I were floating. It was low and heavy, quiet and oppressive.

There is no right way to grieve.

You might cry uncontrollably, or not at all. You might feel numb, or have senses so heightened it hurts to open your eyes. As time passes, the extremes of that early grief will settle into something more moderate; something that enables you to function.

———

Some months later, I helped my mother clear my father's clothes from their bedroom. I held to my face an Aran sweater he wore throughout my childhood, its scratchy wool reassuringly familiar against my cheek. I reached for a jacket and felt the weight of loose change in the pockets, saggy with overuse. I closed my eyes and imagined the jacket still warm with wear, thrown carelessly over the back of a kitchen chair.

And I cried.

———

It is New Year's Eve. My extended family are descending on us, arriving within minutes of each other in a stream of cars squeezed onto the driveway. There are makeshift beds in every room, for cousins and uncles, sisters and grandparents. Someone has lit a fire, although the house is already warm, and a candle fills the hall with orange and cinnamon. There is champagne in the fridge, ready for this evening's toasts.

Absent friends.

We think of them more at certain times of year, don't we? At Christmas and New Year, perhaps, when family comes together; or in the summer, when you'd go camping or take a trip abroad. It's hard. It will be hard for a while yet.

"Nana's here!" A shout from one of my three teenagers, looking from an upstairs window then pounding down the stairs. I go to the door, and I think—as I often do—how strange it still feels, this shift from child to adult. How I sometimes still feel I am playing house—a girl in an oversized apron, pouring orange juice from a miniature teapot.

But I am closer to fifty than forty now. I have a real house, a real tea set, my own children—practically adults themselves. How far we have all come. My mother starts talking before she's even across the threshold, and I hug her, as a dozen conversations break out around us. Someone opens the champagne—*It's five o'clock somewhere!*—and it's chaotic and noisy and exactly the way we like it.

My mother leans into me, her gaze on the uncles and sisters and cousins; on the laughter and catching-up and belated present-giving. She sees, as I do, the people who are missing from the scene. "Daddy would have loved this," she says. Her eyes shine, and perhaps mine do, too, but that's all. Where once tears might have fallen unbidden, today we can make the choice. We choose to feel the happiness all around us instead.

One day, that choice will be yours, too.

3

I promise the waves of grief that knock you off your feet won't drown you

I was never a strong swimmer. Putting my head underwater made me panic, flailing for the sides and gasping for breath. I must have done it as a child, for the mandatory twenty-five-meter badge, but all I can remember is the bribe of potato chips afterward and the promise that, once I passed, the lessons would stop.

When my children were still toddlers, we took them to the seaside. The beach was more stones than pebbles, sharp on the soles of my feet as we ran to the water's edge. All around us, families splashed in the shallows, and further out, surfers glided in with enviable ease. Every now and then one would crash beneath a wave, their board spinning alone. I would hold my breath until they reappeared, grinning and shaking the salt from their eyes before paddling back out.

My husband scooped a child under each arm and waded into the water, leaving me with two hands free for number three.

"Swimming!" she said with the confidence only a three-year-old can have, and I held her horizontally in the water as she kicked her legs and waved her arms. "I'm swimming!"

The sun was high and I was glad of the children's hats and of the sunglasses I'd remembered to wear. Even so, I squinted to see the rest of the family, alarmed to see how far we'd already drifted away from each other. My husband had the children in too deep—I didn't like it—and I waded toward them to ask him to bring them closer to shore, my little fish still "swimming" by my side. Out of nowhere, the stones shifted under my feet, sweeping my legs from beneath me as a wave caught me sideways. I went under, my arms pushing my little fish up up up, my mouth open in an involuntary gasp of salt water. A blur of shapes and colors; an eerie silence; the sting of a hundred tiny stones on my legs, like skidding off a bike onto gravel.

Then I found my feet. Two seconds, maybe three. No harm done. One soaked child, already over the shock and shouting, *Again, again!* One drenched mother, heart pounding, eyes burning, sick with salt.

"Are you okay?" My husband was laughing, running to help, plucking my sunglasses from the return wave. Now the children were laughing too—*Funny Mummy!*—because it must have been comedy from the outside. Two seconds, maybe three. No harm done. But my heart was still pounding, because one moment I was fine, and the next I was drowning—it felt like I was drowning.

———

I drowned a lot in the first few months after Alex died.

As that first year without him tipped from winter to summer, I busied myself with practical tasks that left little room for thoughts of what might have been. The younger children are, the faster they seem to grow, and Alex's surviving twin—although still tiny—was slowly catching up with his peers. I was in his nursery one day, sorting through piles of clothes he had already outgrown, putting them aside for someone else to make use of.

I found it hard to be in that room. Alex had never been in it, but nevertheless it was his room as much as his brother's. I'd decorated it after my twenty-week scan, sufficiently confident to pull off the receipts from the play mat and the cot mobiles and to wash the sheets for the two cots we'd squeezed at right angles to each other in the tiny space. I painted the walls sunny yellow. It was a Sunday afternoon, Elaine Paige on the radio and my husband downstairs, cooking the roast. I had never been happier.

Around the room, level with the top of the cots, I pasted a frieze of A-to-Z wallpaper, an animal for each letter. I pictured my babies pulling themselves up to see the gorilla and the llama; imagined reciting the alphabet as I dressed the boys. *A is for alligator, B is for bat.*

I found it hard to see the single cot now; hard to see the space where the wooden letters on the door had spelled out a second name. Most of all, I found it hard to be reminded of how happy I once was when it felt like—despite the miracle that was now kicking his legs in front of me—I would never be truly happy again.

"Nana gave you this one," I told him as I pulled out an impossibly small onesie from the drawer. A jumper followed, and I held it against him to check for size. It would do for another couple of weeks, I decided. I rooted through the drawer, reaching to the back, where I knew—to my shame— there were clothes still with labels on, unworn and now too small. I pulled out a plastic bag, and my breath caught.

Inside the bag were two cardigans, knitted in soft blue wool, each with three pearlized buttons. I was crying before I realized, my hands squeezing the bag so tightly the fastenings dug into my palms. The ground was shifting beneath my feet; a wave breaking over my head. Drowning.

Clothes are so often a trigger, aren't they? We remember when they were last worn, remember the way they smelled, how they felt when we hugged the wearer. We associate them with events, with places and people. An old school friend's mother had knitted the cardigans. It was no trouble, she said, she liked to knit. Blue for boys, of course, and identical because twins. She folded them into a sandwich bag and handed them over with a hug, awkward above my baby bump.

"I used a pattern for a three-month-old," she said. "You'll end up with so much newborn stuff, you'll want something they can grow into."

The memory propelled me forward, as though I'd been punched in the stomach, and I folded over the cardigans, my head pressed into the carpet. Beside me, my son kicked his legs in happiness, and I turned my face away so he wouldn't see my tears.

———

Society has become dismissive of the word "trigger," as though it is a tiny thing to be plunged back into the worst moments of your life. It is the right word, I think: *trigger*. It feels like being shot. A sudden, horrifying snap from fine to far from it. A rapid wave, dragging you beneath the surface.

My triggers have been, at various times: babies, twins, hospitals, knitted cardigans, the repetitive beep of a hospital machine (and, once, a reversing truck, which sounded so like a hospital monitor I almost fell in its path). Your own reminders might be less tangible: a season, a color, a scent, a piece of music.

Some triggers are easier to predict than others. We can see the ice is thin; we know that if we step too far onto it, it will give way. We are ready for it. Other times, though, we are caught off guard, not even understanding what we're seeing.

Two or three years after Alex died, I was taking a train to London. I was in the station café, deciding on what to eat, when I felt suddenly cold and shaky, as though I were coming down with something.

It was the cake.

I would have laughed had I not been trembling so much. How ridiculous, that a piece of cake should knock me off balance. It was a particular type of packaged cake, sold in the hospital canteen, to which I had developed an unhealthy addiction during our months in intensive care.

Such tricky moments can't be avoided; not unless we hide away for the rest of our lives (and sometimes that feels like the better option, I know). I try to remember that knowledge is power. Each time we come across a new trigger, we're arming ourselves against future occurrences. Knowing our triggers means we can avoid them or, if that isn't possible, prepare for them. I didn't flinch the next time I saw a piece of fruit cake, because my brain had already braced itself for impact. And it continued to brace itself until it no longer had to.

———

Eight years after Alex died, a woman came up to me at the Saturday market. Several years before, she and her husband had bought our house—the one with the yellow nursery—and as we had stayed in the town, we saw them from time to time. All around us the traders were weighing apples and calling to each other across their stalls. The flower seller's van was a riot of blooms. I had all three children with me, helping me hand out flyers for the literary festival.

"How's the house?" I asked, as though it were a living thing. How I had loved that place; how impossible it had been, in the end, to stay. That house was where we took the phone call that changed our lives, that sent us running for the car, racing for the hospital. So much of our lives had taken place within those four walls; so much happiness, so much heartache.

"We love it," she said. Hesitantly, she took something from her bag. "I...I just ran back to get this." She turned it over in her hands, not yet giving it up. One of my children was tugging at my coat, pointing toward the fruit stand. The woman was still talking. "We turned the nursery into an office after we moved in, and I kept this back. I decided it was probably too early to give it to you, then I saw you today and you look so well, so happy, I went back for it. Here."

It was a section of wallpaper. A sunny yellow frieze, with a toothy tiger and a zebra crossing the road. A gorilla peeling a banana. *A is for alligator, B is for bat.* I waited for the wave to take me under, waited to feel like I was drowning. It didn't happen. Instead, I felt a smile tug at the corners of my mouth as I remembered that Sunday afternoon, all those years ago. I stroked the carefully folded paper.

"Thank you," I said. "This means so much."

It meant more than she knew.

It meant I was getting better.

———

As with any other kind of recovery, setbacks are to be expected, and even so many years on, I can still succumb to an unexpected wave. In spring 2020, the world was in the grip of a pandemic, and I felt myself falling. Our television screens showed endless intensive care units, exhausted medics in scrubs and masks. The *beep beep beep* of life-support machines. The world was united in a collective grief, and within it I tumbled back into mine.

Almost as absurd as cake, the final straw was antibacterial hand gel. How could I have predicted that? All those months of applying it every time we entered intensive care, before and after touching the twins. The posters above the sinks, reminding us how to wash our hands.

And yet despite all that, I thought, *he still got sick.*

Antibacterial hand gel in a pandemic is harder to avoid than a slice of cake in a station café. I needed to break the association with death it held for me. I bought brands that didn't smell of hospitals, decanted them into bottles that didn't look as if they belonged on a ward. I applied copious amounts of rose-scented hand cream. I broke the connection. I got better.

———

It is winter, and I am swimming in a lake in North Wales, frost-tipped trees lining the water's edge. In the summer, teenagers jump from the jetty and dive for coins, but at this time of year, it is quiet. A few years ago, realizing I risked passing my phobia of water on to my children as they learned to swim, I trained myself to put my head underwater. Emboldened, I signed up for lessons and learned how to tilt my body from one side to the other, slicing through the water instead of trying to push against it. I began swimming outdoors. I learned to read the lake, to watch the weather coming off the mountains and predict how the water would feel.

Some days the lake is calm, my easy strokes the only break to the surface. At other times an icy wind comes off the hills, chopping it into angry pieces. I swim upright, like a sea horse, head riding high on each new wave. I am exhilarated by the spray, by the cold, by the sensation of beating the water.

Today, I have misjudged the weather. I have swum to the first buoy—it is too late in the year to swim further—in glassy water, cold as ice. But just as I've found my rhythm, just as I turn for home, the lake sucks up the wind and hurls itself at me. A single, sudden slap in the face. I go under, kick once, twice, to the surface. Splutter. *I'm fine, it's fine, I'll be fine*, I tell myself as my pulse returns to normal.

I swim on. I really am fine. I was never in danger—not with my safety float, with my swimming buddies. It is a reminder, that's all, that the weather can change in a heartbeat, and that the lake is bigger—so much bigger—than me.

———

What I've realized, over the years since Alex died, is that we can't make our triggers disappear, but we can learn to control our reactions to them. We can't stop the waves, but we can become better swimmers, surfacing faster, recovering quicker. We can come up stronger.

4

I promise you will find a way to say goodbye

My son is buried beneath a tree in the churchyard through which I used to walk to school. A cobbled path runs around the church to the elementary school behind, and on the day of Alex's funeral, it felt as though only moments had passed since I was skipping and running and chattering my way to class. I paid little heed back then to the gravestones. They were there for grave rubbings, for decoration, for games of hide-and-seek until we were told off.

I see graveyards very differently now. I look at each stone, stopping to read the inscription, subtracting the years to age the grave's occupant. I imagine what they were like, who they left behind. There is something oddly comforting to me about very old gravestones—the ones that lean precariously, their letters worn away and covered with moss. There's a sense of permanence about them, a reassurance that life has gone on and will continue to go on. I know that just as the ground has long since settled, so has the grief of the people who loved and lost. The occupants of these graves are names on a genealogy chart; apocryphal tales told at family dinners. *Of course, your great-great-grandfather ate a raw egg every morning...*

A fresh grave has none of this comfort. The ground is scarred, the grass still bears the footprints of mourners. A new grave means that somewhere, someone is hurting.

Alex's headstone is simple and small. White granite, with etched letters in gold. *Alexander Edward Mackintosh.* Headstones can't be installed right away—something to do with the ground needing to stabilize—and the interim weeks felt like limbo. I couldn't rest, knowing my son was in a grave marked only by a plastic stake.

A friend's brother, who died when we were all too young, keeps my son company. You might find that fanciful—I would have thought the same at one time. Now I'm comforted by the knowledge that Alex is surrounded by other children; that their parents and siblings perhaps say hello, as I do, to each and every child.

I found it impossibly hard, in the beginning, to visit his grave. The first time I went was the day after his funeral. My feet slowed as I drew closer to the church. I knew I would never again be able to see this place in the way I did when I was at school, or when I walked down the aisle. A place of love had become one of sadness.

I stood by his grave, grief-stricken and bewildered. What was I supposed to do? The movies show figures standing silently, or on their knees, weeping. They show one-sided conversations, updates to the dead on what the family's been doing. I tried to talk but felt self-conscious and artificial, as though there were cameras trained on me. I might have prayed, but any faith I thought I had had disappeared.

Just as I was about to leave, a woman walked by with flowers for another grave. I worried that she had seen me arrive and would think badly of me for leaving so soon. She would not have done, of course. I doubt she even noticed me. Those of us who visit graveyards are too focused on our own mission to concern ourselves with other people's habits. Nevertheless, I stayed another few minutes, my fists thrust in my pockets to stop myself from clawing at the bare soil. He was just there, just a few feet from me. I hadn't wanted to see him at the funeral parlor—I wanted to remember him the way he was when he was alive in my arms—and standing there at his grave, it felt as though all I had to do was reach for him and he would be the same, everything would be the same.

I stumbled from the churchyard and into my car. My heart was too close to the surface, like it might break out, and all I could think about was my baby on his own, my baby underground. I pulled away in tears, the windscreen a blur.

There was a sudden sharp crack. An angry face in the car I'd hit. The sound of blood whooshing in my ears as I fumbled for the door handle.

"Didn't you see me? I was right in front of—" The driver stopped short. "Are you okay?"

I shook my head. I couldn't speak.

"Are you hurt?"

I shook my head again. Pointed to the churchyard and forced out a handful of words. *I was… My son… So sorry. My fault. I'm so sorry.*

I gave her my details and promised to pay for the damage to her bumper, but she never called. She was kinder than she needed to be, and I have never again driven when I've been so upset. The funeral had, in many ways, been a healing experience, but I hadn't been prepared for the finality of it. I couldn't get out of my head the memory of my husband walking down the aisle of the church, carrying our son in a tiny white coffin.

———

The funeral parlor backed onto my parents' place. My father (a pathologist, whose dark sense of humor meant I felt instantly at home when I joined the police) used to joke that when he died, we could simply lob him over the wall to where a flat-roofed extension housed industrial fridges.

A few days after Alex died, we had to make arrangements for his funeral. I have only flashes of recollection from this time, like scenes from a film I half-slept through, waking to find characters mid-conversation, in places to which I never saw them travel. I suspect my parents offered to organize the service, but I know my husband and I would have been resolute in our decision to do it ourselves. We are so powerless, aren't we, in our grief? I found it helped me to do something practical, and there is little more practical—or important—than deciding how best to say goodbye to someone who has died.

Something I remember vividly is going to the funeral parlor. We walked around the corner and knocked on the door, and I looked up at the bedroom windows of my parents' home. I remembered being ten years old, playing jump rope over the other side of the wall. If I thought about my dead neighbors at all back then, it was with exaggerated horror. It never occurred to me to acknowledge the bereaved; I never once imagined them standing as my husband and I were now, carrying a lifetime of love with nowhere for it to go.

"Please, come in." The funeral director had a solemn voice, and I wondered if it was his, or if he put it on for work along with the black suit and tie. I tried to imagine him off duty, raucous and flippant, a twinkle in his eye, like my father. I could not. I thought of the death knocks I had done as a police officer, and how each one had shaken me to the core. How did this man deal with such devastation, hour after hour?

"Most people in your situation," he said, when we were sitting at his burnished desk, in a room that felt more like a lounge than an office, "opt for a small, discreet service."

In our situation?

I stared at the brochure filled with coffins; at the box of judiciously placed tissues. I tightened my fingers around my husband's, the way I had when I'd given birth a few weeks earlier. Was it something to be ashamed of that our baby had lived only five weeks? Should his funeral be small because he was? Because his death wasn't important? Because it was distasteful? I felt a tidal wave of anger at this man's neat world, with its preconceptions and social niceties.

"I think," my husband said, more carefully than I wanted to, "that there are lots of family and friends who would like to pay their respects."

There were. There were grandparents and aunts and uncles; godparents who never got to hold their charge, let alone offer guidance. There were friends who felt our pain almost as keenly as we did ourselves, holding their own children tight, recognizing how narrow the ledge is between here and gone. We needed to be together, singing hymns in thick, choked-up voices.

Like the days surrounding it, I remember only snapshots of the funeral. My husband, carrying Alex's coffin. My brother-in-law, the only one of us strong enough to give a eulogy for a life barely lived. The wind, snatching at the pink hat I'd worn in defiance of the blackness that enveloped us. Most of all, I remember the comfort of having so many friends and family around us, walking with us, in our grief.

——

Funerals aren't for the dead, they're for the living. Unless the deceased has left specific instructions, I strongly believe we should have whatever ceremony gives us what we need. Keep the service small or have carriages drawn by plumed white horses. Have guests wear black or all the colors of the rainbow. Sing hymns, or gospel, or heavy-metal power ballads. Hug and laugh and cry. Celebrate life while we mourn our dead.

I don't remember if we had a wake. Isn't that strange? I have a vivid memory of walking out of the churchyard— unwilling to leave Alex, yet unable to bear it any longer—but afterward is a blank. Did we go back to my parents' house? Stand in the living room drinking wine and passing around sausage rolls? I am ashamed that I don't remember, but grief has torn those days and weeks to shreds. My husband would remember, but I will not ask him. This journey is mine, not his, and these blackouts are as much a part of it as what I can remember. Besides, writing this—reliving it—is painful, and I can't bring myself to talk about it as well.

I know: I told you it would stop hurting. Yet here I am, all these years later, sobbing at my desk, remembering that awful day when my son was lowered into the ground and nothing in my power would bring him back.

Here is the difference: I have *chosen* to feel this way. I've chosen to retrace my steps, to unlock a box I had comfortably laid to rest and take out the contents. I've chosen to turn them this way and that, present them for inspection, analyze, and discuss them. I'm writing this because I think it helps to know that we're not alone. I'm doing it because I hope it might help you to know that, too.

———

As the years passed, I often took Alex's siblings with me to visit his grave. Alex was a part of our family—someone we talked about regularly—and on a practical note, I was rarely unencumbered by children. I found it helpful to have the distraction of looking after them and answering the sort of questions only a child could ask.

"Is he a skellington now?" one of them asked. It was

autumn, and the grass around the children's graves was littered with auburn leaves. I thought of the lock of hair in Alex's baby box and swallowed hard.

"Yes," I said. "I think he must be."

"Harry was a skellington for Halloween."

"I expect he looked wonderful." I couldn't help it: I started crying. I tried so hard not to cry in front of the children, but sometimes it just happened. They looked at me with a mix of alarm and curiosity.

"Poor Mummy," one said. An echo of my own words when one of them fell. *Oops-a-daisy. Mummy will kiss it better.* I smiled brightly and handed them the little watering can I'd brought.

"Why don't you see if you can fill this up. You know where the tap is, don't you?" They trotted off happily, and I let out a long breath, blinking away my tears. I pulled out the weeds around the pansies my mother had planted and tidied the edges of the rectangular bed.

The children had returned. "Present for Alex!"

I stood up. "Did you find—" I stopped abruptly and stared down at three upturned jumpers, the way I'd shown them we could collect blackberries when I hadn't thought to bring a bag. Only these jumpers were filled with trinkets. Fairies and stars; woodland animals and whirling windmills.

"Where did you—" The penny dropped. "Oh God." I

looked at the beautifully tended children's graves around us, denuded of their carefully chosen ornaments. I let out something midway between a gasp and a laugh.

"Mummy better now," my eldest declared. He presented me with a small china angel, as though I had scraped my knee and had earned a lollipop for my bravery.

We put back the ones we could remember. The others we lined up by the edge of the children's garden, with a note I'd written on a page torn from my diary. I hoped people understood that my children were doing what children do: collecting what looked like toys, sharing them with their brother.

———

My father wasn't buried but cremated. He hadn't left instructions for what should happen to his ashes, but we were all agreed that he would want to be in Dartmouth, where he had sailed for most of his life, and where the boat he shared with his brothers was moored. Consequently, the following summer saw my father's girls sitting in the stern of the boat with an urn and a bottle of champagne.

"How do you want to do this?" I asked my mother. Until then, our discussions had been focused on the logistics of getting all four of us in the same place at the same time, rather than on the ceremony of the scattering. I tried to think what my father would have wanted.

My older sister said a prayer. We each shared something small about him—something we missed, something we'd always cherish. We cried a little. It was time.

"Ready?" My younger sister took the lid off the urn and held it out, beyond the boat. Sunlight glistened on the water and I watched the gulls glide above us and thought how perfect this place was. There was a light breeze, but we were facing the right way (I had heard comically awful stories of ashes blown in the faces of stricken mourners), and I liked the idea of my father flying above the water, particles carried this way and that before landing in the ocean.

"Ready."

She tipped the urn, but instead of the pretty scattering of ashes I'd envisaged, there was a dull *plop*.

"What was that?"

As one, we leaned over the boat, causing it to lurch alarmingly to one side.

"Oops."

Unbeknown to us, inside the pretty urn, my father's ashes had been placed in a sealed plastic bag, which was now floating on the surface of the water.

"Get it back!"

"We can't get it back."

"We have to! It's pollution. And it's Daddy."

There was a frantic scramble of boat hooks, some *Hold my*

legs!, and a lot of *Don't fall in!*, and my father's sodden ashes were plonked unceremoniously into the cockpit. There was a moment's silence, then my mother started to laugh. One by one, we joined her, until we were beside ourselves with hysteria, tears streaming down our faces. My dad would have adored it.

We are often encouraged to look upon the funeral or the scattering of ashes as our opportunity to say goodbye, but I think grief presents us with a series of goodbyes. Many of us want to keep our lives—our homes, our routines—as close as possible to the way they were before. It helps us feel connected to the person we've lost. When we feel able to change things—to move the chair they always sat in, or eat dinner at a time that never would have suited them—we are saying a small goodbye. We're moving on. In time, we might move house, remarry, have more children; each milestone another farewell.

None of this can be rushed. Well-meaning friends might gently suggest that it's time to clear out your loved one's belongings, but it's time when *you* think it's time. When you're ready to say that particular goodbye. My mother-in-law drew great comfort from knowing her husband's clothes would be worn again. In contrast, a friend keeps her daughter's bedroom exactly as it was the day she died, right down to the pile of clean laundry on the bed, waiting to be put away. Several times in the first ten years after my son died, I packaged up the tiny onesies he had worn, to donate them to the neonatal intensive care unit. Premature baby clothes are expensive and hard to find, and I knew they would be gratefully received. On every occasion, I changed my mind. Eighteen years on, they are still in a bag at the top of my wardrobe—a goodbye I'm just not ready to say.

———

There's a wedding party coming out of the church. I stay out of the way, sitting on a bench by the duck pond while the photographer works. She positions the bride and groom under the lych-gate where my husband and I stood twenty years ago.

When they're gone, the narrow roads around the church suddenly empty of cars, I go to see Alex. Some years ago, they felled the huge tree above his grave. I was sad at first—I'd come to see it as a protector—but I'm used to it now. Things change.

I'm armed with gardening tools and headstone cleaner in a somber bottle. I kneel on my jacket and get to work. I haven't been here for some months—we live more than 150 kilometers away now—and the edges of the grave are ragged and full of weeds. I tidy them up, then rake over the soil. These practical tasks are how I spend time with my boy. Not talking, not telling him my news, not crying for what might have been. Just quietly busying myself with a washing-up brush, bringing up the gold letters till his name shines bright.

There will come a time when the care of this little plot will pass to my children. To Alex's twin brother, whose fingers were once entwined with his, and to the younger siblings he never met.

One day, many years from now, no one will come. The grass will grow over the patch of earth, and the white granite will darken to gray as the seasons leave their mark. The corners of the stone will lose their sharpness, and lichen will soften its faces. The engraved letters will no longer be gold.

There will, perhaps, still be a school here. The children will race along the cobbled path and play hide-and-seek behind the graves, until they're told to stop. Someone will teach them how to hold paper against the stones and rub wax crayon over the letters until they magically appear. *Alexander Edward Mackintosh.*

And someone like me—a grief survivor, years on from their loss—will be comforted by this old, listing headstone in the children's garden. They will see how it has settled into its coat of wild flowers and grass, and how the birds peck at insects in the thick moss that warms the stone. Life has gone on and will continue to go on, and just as the ground has long since settled, so has the grief of the people who loved and lost here.

We're told that funerals and memorial services bring closure, and if that's your experience, I'm truly glad for you. But if the funeral of your loved one brought more pain than peace, you're not alone. If you couldn't have the send-off you wanted, or that they deserved, there are other ways to close that chapter and move forward. A goodbye is more than a funeral or a wake. It's when you move away from the house you shared together; it's the birth of another child. It's getting married again or booking the holiday you always meant to take together. It's moving clothes from the wardrobe to the attic. It's all the times we remember them, then set that memory aside. A goodbye is more than a moment, and you'll find the right time—and the right way—to say yours.

5

I promise you will find a reason to keep going

After Alex died, I didn't want to go anywhere. I wanted to be screwed into a ball in the corner of an empty room. I wanted to howl and have the echoes of my pain thrown back at me, over and over until it deafened me.

I might have stayed that way for days. Weeks, even. Perhaps, if I hadn't had a reason to keep breathing, I might have stopped entirely. It felt like a small step between death and the living nightmare in which I found myself.

But I did have a reason.

There is always a reason.

The nurses had moved our surviving son to another room so we didn't have to see the space where Alex had been. The wind stung my face as we walked across the car park, and my heart thrummed a warning on my ribs.

In the corridor outside neonatal intensive care, I stopped. "I don't think I can do this."

My husband squeezed my hand. "We have to."

We had to.

We had another child on the other side of that door, a child whose condition was still critical, whose future was uncertain. On the other side of that door was our reason.

I kept my eyes on the floor as we walked through the ward, not wanting to see where we'd said goodbye to Alex. The air was thick with the cleaning products I will always associate with grief, the desk staffed with sympathetic smiles.

"I'm so sorry," said a nurse we'd come to know well, who hadn't been on duty the day before. I wondered how many times she'd arrived at work to find that one of the babies had died. She was so gentle with us, so kind. They were all so kind.

Our surviving son was in a small room off the main ward. The nurse fetched a screen so we could shut ourselves away and begin to adjust to the new shape of our family. The screen wobbled, and the blue and green fabric didn't quite cover the frame, but I was grateful for this illusion of privacy. I was shaking so violently I had to sit down, the nurse presenting my baby to me as though I'd just given birth.

He was still light as a newborn, and so much like Alex I almost couldn't bear it. I made myself look at him, made myself seek out the differences—the hair, the tilt of his nose. He was beautiful. In my arms was my reason to live. I knew that. But I felt something else, too—something I was too scared to voice.

I didn't know if it would be enough.

———

For most people, the act of staying alive is a passive one. They leave their bodies to do what is required of them—pumping blood, taking in air and expelling it again—while they get on with their daily lives. When they are well (physically and mentally), they give little thought to what is keeping them in the world.

When we are grieving, we are not well.

I wasn't well for a long time. I became hyper-aware of my mortality, immediately conscious of anything off-kilter, like a diabetic in tune with their insulin needs. Merely being alive felt like a precarious state, my condition frequently tipping into critical. It was as though my oxygen supply was restricted, my central nervous system shutting down. When we're grieving, our bodies don't function normally, and neither do our minds.

Sometimes it's too painful to be alive, isn't it? I understand. I've stood on the edge and looked down into oblivion and thought, *This would be easier*, and perhaps it would have been. I never took that last step forward. My surviving baby needed me, and I needed him, although—of course—it isn't as simplistic as that.

At least you still have your other son. I must have heard a version of this well-intentioned platitude a hundred times. Perhaps to the casual observer, with no personal experience of grief, it feels like the truth. How convenient to have another baby—a near-identical replacement, no less—to lessen my loss!

It doesn't work like that, though. One sibling is no substitute for another; one parent is still half what you had. The widowed you may well marry again, but it won't erase your earlier love. Loving other people doesn't make it easier to lose someone; it simply gives you a reason to keep going.

My son was my reason, and later my other children. My husband, too; our parents, my sisters, my friends; the knowledge that they were there to catch us when we fell, that they carried us through our grief. I was lucky to have them.

Your reason might not be a person. Indeed, if the person you've lost was the very center of your world, if you and they enjoyed a love that eclipsed all others, you will feel so very alone right now. It might feel as though there's no point, no purpose, that nothing will ever be right again. All I can do is tell you to hold on: there are better times ahead, I promise.

In the meantime, you could find it useful to focus on

something practical—a reason to get out of bed each day, a reason to be here in the world. It might sound trite, but I found that thinking of ways to help other people made me feel better. A few days after Alex died, I set up a fundraising page in support of meningitis research. The need to make a difference is so common among those of us who are bereaved that I now instinctively look for details when I hear that someone has passed away. The simple act of donating some spare change is often the only practical way friends are able to help, to ease the symptoms of their own grief as well as yours. Watching the total donations creep up, knowing we are contributing toward a cause that will help prevent a similar tragedy happening to someone else, is a powerful reason to keep going.

You might find that raising money for a cause important to you—or to the person who died—will give you some direction in this rudderless time. The fundraising itself can take many forms. If you're the active type (and if the associated training or exertion provides a useful focus), you could run a marathon or jump out of a plane, climb a mountain or enter a triathlon. If, like me, even getting out of your pajamas each morning feels overwhelming, setting up a donation page is enough. Collecting loose change in a jar is enough. You don't have to launch a charity or march on congress to make a difference.

Closer to home, there might be elderly neighbors to check on, or voluntary work to do, and if you're ready to take on that sort of responsibility, it could help you as much as it helps them. Supporting others gives us perspective and a sense of achievement at a time when we feel so out of control.

Of course, for many of us there are long periods when we're barely capable of dressing ourselves, let alone running errands for someone else. We're the ones who need supporting, the ones suddenly as dependent as children. There is strength in helping others, but there's strength, too, in recognizing when we've reached our limits.

When we lose someone after a long and fulfilling life, there is comfort to be drawn from the memories made together. We recall the adventures we had, and when we feel strong enough, we can have more, in remembrance. I often imagine how my father would feel about the choices I've taken, the life I've made. I am so like him, in so many ways, and that alone feels like a good reason to keep going.

It is harder when we lose someone young, because it is so unjust, and because we don't have those years and years over which to fondly reminisce. Death can be both a cruelty and a kindness, but when someone is very young, it rarely feels like the latter. My son was just five weeks old when he died, having never seen the outside of a hospital ward. There were no stories to share, no *Do you remember when…* prompts for misty-eyed conversations. This might feel familiar to you if you have lost a baby, or if your relationship with the person who died was not straightforward. An absent parent, an estranged partner, a sibling with whom you did nothing but argue. You might feel untethered, with few happy memories to which to moor your grief.

When we can't look backward, we have to look forward. My grief for Alex isn't bound up in memories of his life but in the opportunities he never experienced. If I shut down from the richness the world has to offer, it isn't just one life lost but two. We owe it to the dead to live the lives they didn't get to finish.

———

Soon after Alex died, I was given a gratitude journal. It was a simple notebook with space on each page to write the date followed by three prompts: reasons to be grateful that day. Reasons to keep going. The theory is that by forcing ourselves to search for the bright spots in the darkness, gratitude will eventually become a habit.

Write down anything, devotees say: *a beautiful tree you've seen, a cup of tea with a friend, a good night's sleep.*

I would love to tell you that this journal helped me find my reasons to live, but I also want to be honest with you, and the truth is: I hated that gratitude journal with a passion. Every page—with its neatly boxed-off spaces—was a stark reminder of what *wasn't* there, what I *wasn't* grateful for. Anything I put felt meaningless, followed by an unwritten "but."

The sun shone, I wrote. *But my child is still dead.*

I saw my sister today. But my child is still dead.

How could anything I wrote balance out what had happened?

It was a long time before I realized I'd been trying for the impossible. Nothing can balance out what's happened to us. We shouldn't even strive for it, because we'll forever fail and, in failing, feel worse.

Noticing the good things in life isn't about balancing out the bad; it's about reminding us why we're here. It's seeing the sunrise and realizing you want to see another; hugging a friend and carrying the warmth of that hug home. It's noticing the spring leaves unfurl, or spending an hour on the sofa just because the cat is asleep on your lap.

These reasons to keep going are all external—influences from the world around you, reminding you there is still happiness to be had—but there is a reason closer to home.

You.

You are already someone's reason to keep going. You are a line in someone's gratitude journal, a moment of joy in their day. You have already made a difference, and you have many more to make.

You are your reason.

6

I promise this won't always be your first thought in the morning

I woke before the alarm. It was perhaps three weeks after Alex died, although time played tricks on me back then. *I need to put a wash on*, I thought, my eyes still sticky with sleep. *The boys will need clean clothes and—*

The *boy*.

The *boy* will need clean clothes.

A splinter of pain, like losing him all over again; like coming back from a punch only to end up on the ropes again. It is the worst kind of déjà vu, when sleep has been mercifully free of nightmares and you wake with the clarity of a sunny morning after a storm. Everything feels fresh and new, as though you've been reborn.

And then you remember.

I made a sound, somewhere between an *oh* and a cry, and reached for my husband as he woke, dragging him back into the ring. Outside, it was still dark, sodium-yellow street light filtering through the window. It was December—or perhaps January—but the heating had not been on for weeks. We were at the hospital from seven in the morning till ten each night most days, and there seemed little point in warming an empty house. Perhaps on some level, we were punishing ourselves, the same way we ate cardboard canteen sandwiches instead of fresh rolls from the deli—both options an identical walk from the ward. It felt wrong to have nice things when one son was in hospital, the other in the ground.

Oh. My cry misted in the air, a physical manifestation of my grief.

"I know," my husband said. "I know."

"I can't take this." *This.* This crushing pain in my chest, this sensation of drowning, my brain's constant attempts to turn back time. The cruel act of remembering, each morning.

"I know," he said. "I know."

There are many reasons why shared grief can be hard (more on this later), but it is a quiet relief to be with someone who feels your pain as intensely as you do, who needs no explanation for why, suddenly, it hurts now.

I met my then police officer husband at work, an occupational hazard common to emergency service workers. It is, in part, the unsociable hours and the intensity of the work that draws colleagues together, but it is also a desire to be with someone who truly understands the pressures of the job. For a while, my husband and I worked on the same team, but even after we moved to separate departments, we still spoke the same language.

"Nasty fatal today," he'd say, hanging his coat on the peg by the front door. "Family of four."

I'd nod and squeeze him tight and know that if he wanted to talk, he would. I didn't need to ask questions. I knew what that scene on the motorway might have looked like, how it felt to be too late to help. I knew the physical exhaustion, the emotional toil. I knew, too, that this was part of the job, and tomorrow he—and I—would do it all over again.

Now we had added grief to our shared lexicon.

We lay in bed, the duvet too warm and the room too cold, and let silence fill the space around us. There was nothing to say, because nothing could make it better. Another morning, another reminder.

Some days, realization would come fast, slamming against me the second I opened my eyes. *He's dead, he's dead, he's dead.* A punch to the stomach before I'd had a chance to brace. Other mornings, I'd feel a quiet but insistent uncertainty. It crept into the early-morning peace, like the unsettled feeling of perhaps having left the gas on or forgotten to lock the door.

What is it? What happened?

Oh.

He's dead, he's dead, he's dead.

On the worst mornings, I woke in the full, awful knowledge of what had happened, as though my mind had been poised, gleefully, to remind me the second I was awake.

He's still dead, you know.

Whichever way the day started, my first thought was of Alex. Or, more accurately, of the loss. My son's absence was a black hole, sweeping all surrounding matter into its depths. It would be this way forever, I was sure; and I was sure, too, that I wanted it so. Because he was the center of my world, and if I didn't hold him in my head, I might lose him in my heart.

It's a hard way to start each day, isn't it?

I remember reading an interview with some celebrity who outlined his daily routine in intimidating detail. *I start each day by meditating,* he said, *then I drink a kale smoothie and work out...*

I stared at the page, at the photograph of this man who spoke a different language to me.

I start my day by remembering my son is dead, I thought. *Then I lie there, my throat tight with the effort of trying not to cry, and I attempt to turn back time. I relive the day he died, minute by minute, trying to step into the moment and change what happened next.*

Sometimes I would dream that Alex was alive. That he was sleeping in the next room, with his twin brother. I would scoop them up, one in each arm, and carry them downstairs. We would be at the park or in the car on our way to an adventure. Once I dreamed my boys had grown up, and it was so real that when I woke, I expected to see an old woman in the bathroom mirror. The mind games grief played on me made me feel as though I were going mad.

For years after my father died, I would pick up the phone to call him. I would hear a daft joke and think, *I must tell him that*, before realizing with a jolt that he was no longer here. There was nothing wrong with my memory—I certainly hadn't forgotten he was dead—so why did my mind play such a cruel trick, over and over?

As the years passed, I learned to reframe these moments. My mind was not *taunting* me but *treating* me. It was reminding me that yes, he would have laughed at that joke, he would have loved hearing that news. The memories came with a sharpness that took my breath away, but over time, the sharpness became fleeting, like the cold shock of a swimming pool before you acclimatize.

It is a gift to be reminded of the ones we love. It is through these moments that they live on.

———

I wake before the alarm. It is September, and I have three teenagers who are becoming adults before my eyes. *Waffles,*

I think. *I will make waffles* (it is still early in the school year; by February I will be pushing toast at them as they pull on their shoes). I think about the vegetable patch I haven't weeded, and where I might walk the dogs today. I mull over a character in the novel I'm writing. I get up and feed the dogs, wake the teens, mix batter, find gym clothes, open the mailbox, see everyone off to school.

When the house is quiet, I turn on my laptop, where this book is waiting for me.

And that's when I think about my boy.

I open the box of memories and let them tumble out—those early weeks of despair, the months of pain, the years of sorrow—and I analyze my grief. How different it is after so many years. It's like looking through a photo album, recognizing the person in that faded photograph, yet finding it hard to reconcile them with who they are now. The same smile, perhaps, although even that has changed a little. And everything else—the clothes, the hair!—is so wildly different. And yet, underneath, still the same. The same, but different.

One day, you will wake up and your first thought will not be one of sadness. You will think how the mornings are getting lighter, or how it is surely far too early for neighbors to be mowing the lawn. You will curse yourself for forgetting to put the trash out, regret that last glass of wine, or wish you'd stayed for one more. You will roll over and go back to sleep, or swing your legs from under the covers and go to make tea. You will not wake up staring grief in the face.

Grief makes us feel as though we're losing our minds, but I think what we lose is control over our thoughts. Grief takes the wheel from us, directing our focus toward what we've lost, leaving us disempowered and overwhelmed, out of control. We think of our loved one the second we wake because they were the most important person in our life and their death has shaken our very existence. We think of them because grief needs an outlet and, in our barely awake state, we don't have the resources to control it.

You will find those resources, I promise.

You will grow strong again, able to focus your mind on what you have, not what you've lost. You will gently set aside your memories, to get on with your day, or because it is not the right moment to relive them. You will be back in control of your thoughts, grief merely a passenger, not the driver.

7

I promise you won't always fear the worst

I stood on the landing, the floorboards creaking slightly as I shifted my weight from one foot to the other. My hand closed around the doorknob. In a moment, I'd open the door. I just needed a little more time to prepare.

It was seven in the morning, and I was waking my five-month-old, because no matter what people say about never waking a sleeping baby, we had a routine, and the routine worked. Whenever I am overwhelmed by life—because of grief, or workload, or the awfulness of the news—I instinctively seek out structure. A morning alarm. A cup of tea at ten. Three meals a day. I have always written a daily to-do list, and when I look back through my desk diaries, I can track my mental health through the length of these lists. The longer the list, and the smaller the tasks—*get up, shower, unload dishwasher*—the more out of control I was feeling.

I was rarely in control in that first year. Creating a schedule for my day meant passing for someone who was holding it together, and the schedule meant waking the baby. Every morning—and after every nap—I stood with my hand on the door, performing a silent ritual I'm almost too embarrassed to share with you.

In a moment, I'll walk in, I'd say to myself, *and he won't be breathing.*

I would play out the subsequent scene—the emergency call, the ambulance, the somber faces of doctors who'd done their best. I'd steel myself against the worst-case scenario, and only when I was certain I was ready would I open the door.

Every morning and after every nap.

For years.

It's only now, telling you about it, that I can see how unwell I was, that in trying to protect myself from what felt like the inevitable, I was spiraling into negative thoughts that won't have helped my recovery. The ritual was preparing me for tragedy, ensuring I was equipped to deal with it, that I wouldn't fall apart. The rest was superstition. *If I'm ready for it, it won't happen.*

As my son grew older, I had to stop myself from calling the doctor for every tiny ailment. Once, before he was walking, I was waiting outside the doctor's office as it opened, pacing anxiously with a bundle of hot baby in my arms. He had a rash. A fever. He wouldn't turn his head.

"I'm sure it's nothing," I told the doctor, although I wasn't sure—not sure at all. The doctor had a photo on her desk of her own children, and I wondered whether she panicked when they fell ill, if she ever googled their symptoms and concluded they were dying.

"Let's have a look, shall we?"

Icy fear was laced around my throat, squeezing tight. I'd pressed a glass to his skin, over and over, till I was seeing spots no matter where I looked. "My elder son had meningitis," I said. "He died, so…" My voice broke.

"So it's extremely important we put your mind at rest," the doctor said. "I understand."

My son was fine. He was always fine. And slowly I started to level out.

———

When my surviving son was six months old, I succumbed to a virus which laid me low for days on end. We had just moved house and were surrounded by boxes, and I'd been unprepared for the emotions of finishing one chapter and starting another. This new house was a fresh start, away from the memories of the one in which we'd become a family of four and then three, but instead of feeling revitalized, I felt exhausted.

After I'd vomited for the third day running, I bought a pregnancy test. We had been told unequivocally that we couldn't fall naturally pregnant, but nevertheless it felt sensible to rule it out. My premature labor—and subsequent emergency surgery—had left me with a significant amount of unresolved trauma, and even doing the test made me sick with fear. *What if it happens again?* How ironic, I thought, that I should feel grateful for our infertility.

The test was positive.

If this were a novel, that moment would be my happy ending. The balm for my grief, the reward for my pain and suffering. At the very least, I would like to tell you it was a joyous moment, but real life is rarely as perfect as fiction.

"What if it's twins again?" I said when I broke the news to my husband.

He did his best to be reassuring. "It won't be. It's a natural pregnancy. This will be fine."

But my glass was half empty, and I was already fast-forwarding to disaster. It would be twins, I knew it. Another high-risk pregnancy, another early delivery, another battle for life. New traumas can trigger old ones, and I slid rapidly backward into grief.

I refused to acknowledge the pregnancy, ignoring my growing belly and eschewing maternity clothes in favor of straining zips and open buttons. What was the point of buying elasticated waistbands when I wouldn't hold on to my babies long enough to get my money's worth? My mental state was such that I was referred for an early scan, to put my mind at rest that I was carrying a single baby, that the stresses and strains under which my body had been placed during my previous pregnancy would not occur this time. My mind was a maelstrom of worst-case scenarios—all of which felt entirely rational. The baby would have a disability incompatible with life. I would, once again, have insufficient amniotic fluid to keep it safe. I would bury another child. As I lay down for my ultrasound, I waited to be told there was no heartbeat.

There were two.

"You were right," the sonographer said, once she had recovered from the shock. "You're having twins again." Being right was the worst possible thing that could have happened. If I was right about it being a twin pregnancy, I reasoned, I would be right about its outcome.

"They're going to die," I said, to my husband, the health visitor, the midwife, friends. I was clinical and cold, terrified and—quite possibly—terrifying. My consultant added weight to my fears with frightening statistics, setting the chances of a live birth at around 30 percent. I was to have surgery to improve those odds; I was forbidden from picking up anything heavier than a kettle—including my own son.

I just wanted it over. It seemed to me—in my broken, grief-stricken, mixed-up mind—that if lightning were going to strike twice, it would be better for it to hit now than for me to live in this fearful state for another seven months.

———

In February 2008, my second set of twins arrived safely, fifteen months after the first, and with a combined weight of almost thirteen pounds. I'd been wrong. Lightning did not strike twice.

———

For most people, death is an unlikely event. It's something that happens to strangers, in other places, other lives. They think of it fleetingly, in abstract ways, if at all.

It's different for us, isn't it?

We know.

We know how fragile life is, how someone can be here one moment and gone the next. We are acutely aware of danger, a part of us always braced for bad news. It becomes entirely possible that your sister might go to work one day and not return, that your father could drop dead crossing the street. We've been through the worst. We know that terrible things happen, so what's stopping them from happening again?

It is, I have realized, okay to be a little neurotic after experiencing the death of someone close to us. People understand it. Expect it, even. They are, mainly, supportive and sympathetic. I try to analyze my feelings, to work out if my reaction is proportionate. Is it reasonable to fear illness when all the indicators suggest someone is sick? Yes, absolutely.

Is it reasonable to fear that a bus might plow into your loved one as they walk quite safely on the pavement, a barrier between them and the road? Is it rational to stand on the landing every morning, one hand on the doorknob, preparing for your child to be dead?

I gently suggest that it isn't, and if I had my time again, I might have found someone to help me unpack my compulsion to anticipate the worst-case scenario. Pessimism plagued me for years, and it wasn't confined to my own life. When friends excitedly shared news of their pregnancies, I had to bite my tongue. I knew how inappropriate it would be to articulate the negativity in my head, but my immediate instinct was to imagine the worst. Every holiday could end in disaster, every wedding felt laced with risk. I had to force myself to look forward to birthdays, or anniversaries, ignoring the voice in my head that said: *That day might never come.* Grief was my own grim reaper, looming over happy times, reminding me how easily they could be snatched away.

I know what you're thinking: I must have been fun at parties, right?

But grief turns us all into actors. We smile and we laugh, so long after our loss that no one else even thinks of it; they would never imagine that inside we're thinking more about death than life. Grief is the riptide in our seemingly calm sea.

———

It is Saturday, almost one in the afternoon. I wake up the teens, because honestly, how can anyone sleep for so many hours? They are practically nocturnal. I march up the stairs and throw open three doors: *bang, bang, bang.* "Morning!" I sing cheerfully because it infuriates them. I pick up strewn socks and deposit them on pillows in the hope that it might encourage discovery of the laundry basket. I pull open blinds and lift sash windows, and the teens groan and pull the covers high over their heads. I go back downstairs, mumbling about how it would be nice to see some activity before the sun goes down, and I suppose I'm doing the dishwasher on my own again, am I? I think about what might be lurking under beds and in drawers, and I contemplate asking them to strip their sheets. I remind myself to book dentist appointments and order school blazers.

Never once does it cross my mind that they could ever be anything but gloriously, brilliantly, wonderfully alive.

8

I promise you won't always feel so angry

I was in the kitchen when I heard the postman pull up. He left the door of his van open, as he always did, Radio 1 blaring into the morning with ferocious chirpiness. I hadn't slept well—when did I ever sleep well?—and was still in my pajamas as I cleared up the detritus left from breakfast. At the soft slap of envelopes on the mat, I went into the hall to collect the mail. Along with a couple of bills and a postcard from my sister was a Royal Mail card.

Sorry we missed you.

"Sorry you missed me?" I said. "I'm right here!" I opened the front door and stepped outside in my slippers. "Excuse me!" But the radio was loud and the postman was late, and the red van disappeared up the hill.

I slammed the front door. "I was right here!"

The card said I would get my parcel tomorrow, or I

could collect it myself, but not until after 2:00 p.m., when, presumably, the postman would have finished his round. I had no idea what was in it—I wasn't expecting anything—but somehow that made my frustration ten times worse. It could be important. Even if it wasn't, it was *my* parcel, and he hadn't even *tried* to deliver it. Hadn't even bothered to knock! I stomped back to the kitchen and extracted the children, ushering them up the stairs and snapping unfairly when they were slow. Despite the coolness of the morning, the back of my pajama top clung to my spine as my own temperature rose. What should have been a minor irritation had assumed monumental proportions.

"How dare he?" I muttered, wrenching tights over recalcitrant limbs. "Who does he think he is?" With no other adult home to moderate my rage—to make a joke of the annoyance—it festered inside me as I played shop with the children, as I chopped fruit for their snack. As they napped, I paced, holding angry conversations in my head and texting my husband to say, *You won't believe what the postman did this morning.* By 2:00 p.m., the rage inside me was out of control. I put the kids in the car—a harder task than it sounds—and drove to the sorting office, where I jangled my keys in the queue and sighed loudly when the man in front took too long to produce his ID.

"He didn't even knock!" I said, when it was my turn.

"I'm sorry about that." The man behind the counter looked tired. He might well have been genuinely sorry, but I was far beyond the point at which I could recognize that. I continued to rant about the hapless postman—his choice of radio station and the volume at which he listened to it—along with the Royal Mail in general and the state of Britain today as I thrust my driving license across the counter. I'd like to think I had the grace to thank the man for my package (which contained nothing of significance); I know he must have rolled his eyes at my departure.

This disproportionate, unnecessary anger went hand in hand with my grief for a very long time. It has arrived in waves, just as grief itself has. It has left me exhausted and empty, just as grief has. I've been angry in ways that are perhaps understandable (with neglectful parents; with God; with a GP receptionist who rang to book vaccinations for a child who had died a year before), and in ways that make no sense at all (at a stubbed toe, a key that wouldn't turn, a barista who misheard my name). I have been angry for weeks at a time, so permanently irritated it became my entire personality, until even I couldn't bear to be with me. I had always valued tolerance, and considered myself to be balanced and empathic, yet for years I was fierce and dismissive, intolerant of anxieties I considered to be petty when compared to my loss.

It's easy to see now that my anger was never really directed at the postman or the Royal Mail, at the barista, or at the chair leg on which I stubbed my toe.

I was angry because my son had died.

———

A short walk from our house was a family center—playgroups, a nursery, drop-in coffee mornings, that sort of thing. When I first walked in there, I was reeling from the news that I was pregnant again. I was unsteady on my feet, my eyes unnaturally wide, like a survivor leaving a crash site. Clasped to my hip was my eight-month-old son, small enough for newborn diapers and still needing specialist care. Written in red on my calendar, among the baby massage and Sing & Sign dates, were appointments with physios and cardiac specialists. It felt never-ending.

"We were in special care, too," a woman said as we swapped stories over coffee. I smiled at her baby, bonny and blithe, and the woman shook her head. "No, my daughter. She died." Everything else—all the other parents, the staff, the running toddlers, and the crying babies—disappeared. It was just me and another woman who knew the pain I was going through. We could be friends, I thought. We would help each other through grief and become stronger.

"What was her name?" I asked, because that should always

come first. As she spoke, I pictured this child, who had lived for many years more than mine. There had been complications in hospital; she had been left with brain damage not dissimilar to that suffered by my son.

There, our paths diverged. The woman's daughter went home, to live a life in one room, a life being shuffled from bed to chair to bath and back. I could only imagine how hard it had been, yet I was still envious of this other mother.

"Are you suing?" she asked, as easily as if she were asking what supermarket I shopped in.

I frowned. "Why would I sue?" The rest of the room came back into focus. A baby smiled on his mother's lap, her tea held carefully away from his curious fingers. On the wall, brightly colored charts counted apples and buttons and cars.

"Your son contracted a hospital bug. If they were negligent…"

"I don't think they were."

"You won't know unless there's an investigation. I'd be demanding an investigation. That's what I'm doing."

"It was no one's fault." I wanted the conversation to end.

"It's always someone's fault," she said grimly. She recommended legal firms, talked of lawyers who'd refused her case and others who gladly took her money. She spoke of her battle to simply make someone listen; of hearings and appeals, meetings and arguments spanning one year to the next. As she spoke, I sensed the fury built inside her. Like flint on stone, love and grief together seemed to have sparked a blaze of anger, an unstoppable force that consumed her entire life.

Afterward, I walked home. It was a crisp autumn day, leaves crunching on the pavement and spilling onto the road. Was Alex's death someone's fault?

Should we have sued?

I felt somehow less of a mother that I wasn't dedicating my life—and my life savings—to establishing the cause of my son's death. What that woman had described sounded exhausting: a relentless, all-consuming fight for answers that might not ever be found. My own bursts of anger were short-lived—sprints, not marathons—and I wasn't sure I had the space for such sustained levels of rage. What difference would it make to win a court case? To establish that Alex had died because someone had failed to do their job properly? It wouldn't bring him back to me.

In the end, my reluctance to battle with the authorities wasn't because it seemed pointless, or because I feared we would lose. It wasn't that I didn't have the strength for a marathon. It was because I wasn't angry with them. I knew the hospital staff hadn't been negligent, that they'd done everything they could to save Alex's life when the odds were stacked against them. I knew that without them I wouldn't be pushing an eight-month-old home from the family center.

———

Sometimes grief turns itself into anger without us noticing, and we have to work hard to interrupt the process before we take it out on people who don't deserve our wrath. On other occasions, I think it is a more conscious decision. It can be easier to channel feelings into anger than to allow them out in choked sobs; it feels more productive to obsess over supreme court case studies than to lie in bed waiting for the world to end. Society accepts anger more readily than grief.

It does happen, of course, that someone dies due to someone else's actions—or inaction. When I was a police officer, I delivered such horrific news to more people than I can count; the lives of their loved ones lost to industrial accidents, to road traffic collisions, to assaults and murder. I am so sorry if, out of everything in this book, this is what speaks to you. I can't imagine how awful it must be, how angry you must be with those responsible.

I think that, just as we cannot hide from grief (it will find us, eventually), we have to lean into our rage. If something makes you angry, be angry! Your emotions are valid and real and nothing to be ashamed of. Maybe there are chapters in this book that have made you want to hurl it across the room, and that's fine, the book can take it. Better out than in, as they say, because I think that suppressed anger eats away at us in the same way grief does, and makes us desperately unhappy.

Whether our rage is justified or irrational, it has to go somewhere. I've always felt we have two options: help it to dissipate gently, or let it out in a burst. I confess I've always defaulted toward the latter. If you're a gentler person than I am, you might try breathing exercises, which direct your focus away from whatever intense emotion it is you're feeling. You can count as you breathe (in for four seconds, hold for seven, out for eight), or simply spend a few minutes breathing slowly and deeply, thinking of nothing but each inhalation and exhalation.

When you need to let rip (and we all do, sometimes), it's helpful to find outlets that absorb our rage instead of reflecting it back at us; a punching bag instead of a friend, a scream in a car instead of an argument with a cashier.

Several years after Alex died, I felt a burning inside me as I inched forward on a beltway snarled up with traffic. It struck me that anger felt very much like grief in the way it rose like flood water; that anxiety, too, behaved in the same insidious way. Unlike cheerfulness or joy—which can land in an instant—these uncomfortable emotions seep through our veins and drown us from the inside. By the time I reached open roads, golden fields stretching on either side, I could barely breathe. I was not angry with the traffic, or with the difficult day I'd had at work; I was angry with life. Angry with whatever twist of fate had given my son an infection, had made that infection take over every part of his brain. Angry that he had died when others lived; that his death was a moment, yet my grief would last forever. Angry that I still felt this way, after so much time.

Alone in the car, away from the traffic, I screamed. The sort of scream that would bring people running, that would scare dogs and frighten children. A scream that belonged in horror movies and murder mystery dinners. I recommend it.

When I got home, I put on my trainers and went for a run, something I always find dissolves tension. I dislike running, which makes it an excellent activity on which to take out my anger (although I hear it's an equally effective stress reliever if you love it). The closest loop to our house could be done in two directions, and I opted for the steeper climb to make my lungs burn. It was dark, the insides of the houses I passed looking cozy and warm, and I let my resentment fuel my steps. I ran faster than I could sustain, stopping at the top of the hill to lean on a gate and take deep gulps of air. Beneath me, the town twinkled and the air was still, and the fire inside me had burned itself out.

Anger willingly allows itself to be channeled into physical exertion, and if you have the ability to run, or swim, or punch a bag, you might find it helps. For some, the salve comes in the form of loud music or meditation, a comedy podcast or a night out with friends. Your anger is unique to you, just as your grief is unique to you.

Of all the ways I've found to deal with my anger, the most effective is simply to acknowledge it. To myself and, sometimes, to others.

"I'm disproportionately angry about it," I say to my husband when something has tipped me over the edge. Almost instantly, I feel better. Acknowledging an emotion is the first step in understanding it, and recognizing its irrationality removes its power.

"Is there anything I can do to help?" he asks, because it is a regular occurrence, and because he recognizes the sensation better than most.

"I don't think so."

"Okay." He stands close enough to touch, a not-quite-a-hug. Shoulder to shoulder, both figuratively and literally.

"I'm just…" I flounder, unable to find the words, settling simply for: "I'm just so angry."

"I know." And he does, of course.

Maybe you do, too.

—

I live in a small town now, where everyone knows everyone. Our doorbell rings constantly. Kids calling for mine to come out; friends popping over for a brew. Neighbors needing a favor, or dropping back something they've borrowed. From my study on the second floor, I have advance notice of visitors and can holler to the teens to answer the door. The delivery drivers are mostly for me. Online orders or finished copies of my books for me to marvel at. Sometimes by the time I've got downstairs and corralled the dogs into the kitchen, the postman has gone. I step outside and catch a glimpse of red van as it leaves the drive.

This morning, I missed a delivery entirely. The text message I received reads *Left on porch*, but there's no parcel by the door, so I click on the link to see the proof they've offered. Sure enough, there's a photograph of a box with my name on it nestled safely on a doormat, next to a door. Only it isn't *my* door.

I push my feet into gardening clogs and grab a coat. I make my way down one side of the street and up the other, scrutinizing the photo for clues to the door's owner. Blue…but not that blue. A coir doormat, but plain, not patterned.

I should be working—I have this book to finish, and edits to do on another—and I don't have time to play hide-and-seek. It's annoying, I'm annoyed, and yet…it's just one of those things, isn't it?

Snap! Blue door. Plain mat. No parcel.

I knock. I know who lives here, although not the young man—still half asleep—who opens the door. Yes, he did get a parcel, not long ago; assumed it was for his mum, it's around here somewhere…

I walk home in the rain, the package under my arm. Just one of those things.

———

I would love to tell you that nowadays I am never angry. That I glide serenely through life, never raising my voice, never losing my temper. That I smile beatifically when faced with road rage, take deep breaths when my favorite jumper is shrunk in the wash.

But this is real life, not a fairy tale.

I am not a calm person. I regularly stomp about the house, taking out my frustrations on the vacuum cleaner, the dogs, the front door. I shout at the teens when I'm on deadline and can't find the right words. I lose my temper with the printer, make *What are you doing?* gestures at incompetent drivers, and snap at the supermarket checkout machine: *It is in the bag, you idiot!* In short: I am, I think, a pretty normal forty-something woman with a job, a family, a busy life, and patience that will only stretch so far.

But I no longer have a fuse so short it ignites in an instant. I no longer have rage simmering constantly beneath the surface, like a volcano liable to erupt at any moment. I don't need to find an outlet for anger, because I'm no longer angry my son died. I'm sad. I miss him. I wish things had been different. But I'm not angry, not anymore. It happened, and there is nothing I can do to change that.

It's okay to be angry, just as it's okay to feel sad, to feel happy, to experience the entire spectrum of emotions—sometimes in the same day. Grief is messy and complicated, and some of its symptoms stay with us forever. You won't always feel so angry, but when you do, roll with it. It will pass.

9

I promise you won't always feel so guilty

"It was my fault."

I was sitting with my best friend, my tea going cold on the side. I was still at the stage where I analyzed every action, every moment of what I had come to think of as "before."

"It wasn't your fault."

I don't know how many times she's repeated it over the years. Always with the same level of conviction, never frustrated, never flippant. *It wasn't your fault.*

I began to list the ways.

We'd had fertility treatment. It increased the likelihood of multiple births and, in consequence, the risks; and hadn't I read something, somewhere, about links between IVF and prematurity?

"You can find evidence for anything," said my friend, "if you search hard enough."

And then, attending that baby show in London: all those halls, all those exhibitors. Traipsing around all day, at twenty-two weeks pregnant. All those people, coughing and sneezing over me.

"You could have picked up that bug anywhere."

But I picked it up there. I knew I had, the same way we know the precise meal that made us ill, because when we recall it, our stomach heaves.

The baby fair had been just as you might expect: a vast exhibition hall filled with stallholders persuading overexcited parents-to-be that they needed a bottle warmer, or a diaper bag, or a special syringe for removing mucus from a baby's nose. It was hot and noisy and totally unnecessary, but my God, I loved it. I loved swaying my bump through each new set of doors, examining the map to see which stands were here, what freebies we might pick up. I loved my husband's reassuring hand on the small of my back, hearing the pride in his voice when he told another stallholder: *Yes, it's twins.* When you've been told that you can't conceive naturally—in itself a grief—attending an event specifically for expectant parents feels like a miracle.

I felt nauseous even before we unloaded the car of the double buggy that had been such a bargain (ex-display and non-returnable, but why would we want to return it?), so I went to bed early, exhausted by the day. I woke in the early hours with my stomach in knots; agonizing cramps that sent me rushing to check for blood. I've never been so relieved to vomit. I wasn't giving birth! I was just sick! I was so delirious with relief, I hardly cared that I was too weak to stand. The doctor made a house call—something I thought only happened in novels—and prescribed rest and water. He declared the babies' heart rates strong and steady, and we all relaxed.

"You can't even be certain that's what triggered early labor," my friend said gently.

But I knew.

A fortnight later, I had a routine scan. I'd left work early and driven myself to Oxford, realizing that it wouldn't be long before I'd be too big to fit behind the wheel. In the waiting room, I flipped through a magazine, sizing up the other bumps, guessing how far along they were. I bought an Eccles cake from the hospital café (*Eating for three, actually!*), scattering flakes of buttery pastry on my stomach.

"Mrs. Mackintosh?"

You'll have had moments like this. In a hospital room, perhaps, like me, or in your front room. Taking a phone call from the police, or a relative, or a friend. You'll remember the precise second you heard the news. The moment your life changed. If you close your eyes now, it'll spool out, the scenes as vivid and terrifying as the day they first played.

I had lost my amniotic fluid. I was horrified. How could I have been so careless? How could I have not noticed?

"You'll have lost a tiny amount each day," the consultant explained. "I imagine it's been happening for a couple of weeks. Have you been ill at all?"

I was admitted. Feet up, legs and fingers crossed.

"Next time you leave hospital," the nurse looking after me said, "you'll be taking your babies home."

Baby. As it turned out.

I'm so sorry I didn't keep you safe, I wrote in my diary, over and over, in the weeks that followed.

"It wasn't your fault," my friend said, over and over. Still patient, still gentle.

But even if it wasn't, even if everything that led up to the early arrival of our babies was simply *one of those things*, the final decision to end Alex's life was ours.

There are many times in our lives when we hang in the balance between life and death. The moment we step back from the road, the car seen just in time; the moment we lie on the operating table, powerless in the hands of the surgeon. Such moments are almost always out of our control; rarely do we have a choice. When we do, we live with the consequences forever.

My son died because we chose to turn off the machines that were keeping him alive. We didn't want him to die; we wanted to spare him a life without choices of his own.

Guilt, like grief, cares little for nuances.

It was my fault. That's how it felt.

In my experience, guilt and grief are so closely interwoven it's hard to tell where one ends and the other begins. In the months after my second set of twins were born, I was ridden with guilt for not bonding with them, for not feeling the way I knew a mother was supposed to. It was a long time before I understood that I had loved them from the start; I had simply been protecting myself from what had felt like the inevitable: that one, or both, of them would die. All these years later, I still worry about the impact of those early months.

———

Even if you didn't play a part in death itself, you might feel guilty for the care you should have taken before it was too late. You might feel guilty for words spoken, and for those left unsaid; for the calls you made and didn't make; the bad thoughts you had; the last conversation. If only you'd known.

After my father died, I thought of all the times I'd been secretly bored by his lectures on politics. When he visited me in Paris during a university year abroad, I was mortified by his insistence on packing a hunk of cheddar and a loaf of sliced white bread.

"You can never get a decent sandwich here," he'd said.

What I wouldn't give now for a chat under the Eiffel Tower over a round of cheese and pickle.

We made plans to walk the Welsh coastal path together but never made it beyond looking at a map; we talked about the classic car he'd buy when he retired and how we'd drive somewhere in convoy—him in his TR6, me in my MG Midget. He never got the chance.

———

Guilt over what hasn't been done is a form of self-flagellation that achieves nothing. I think we have to focus on what we *did* do. I remember meeting my dad in the Paris train station, showing him around the city I was then calling home. I think about the epic journey we took from Buckinghamshire to Le Mans, crammed overnight in the Midget because I'd forgotten to book a hotel.

No matter how troubled our relationship with the person we've lost—no matter how brief a time we spent together— there will be moments to treasure. We can direct our energy into remembering what we did, not what we wish we'd made time for.

I had thirty-three years to make memories with my father. I was granted only five weeks with my son, but I remember the surge of elation as I gave birth, the rush of love as I held him for the first time. I remember my confidence growing with each diaper change as he taught me how to be a mother. I wish so much that I'd taken more photographs—that I hadn't waited for him to lose the feeding tube, or wear proper clothes, or leave hospital—but I cherish the few I have.

Find those moments and hang on to them, and when guilt creeps around the corners of your mind, brandish them at your traitorous self. I see your *didn't return her call* and I raise you all the times you had her back. Deal me a *should have known something was wrong* and I'll slap on the table a memory of the good times, of the *I love you*s and the *Haven't we had a great day*s.

If they were still alive, they'd forgive us for whatever minor transgression keeps us awake at night, wouldn't they?

Of course they would.

So we have to forgive ourselves.

———

It is one of grief's great ironies that just as we begin to feel better, guilt slams back to make us feel worse.

How dare you be happy after everything that's happened!

Shortly after Alex died, our neighbors took us to the theater. It was Christmas, and so it was a pantomime, and I had never felt less like going to a pantomime. Our surviving son was still in hospital, and life was a never-ending commute between there and home, sitting beside one bed before driving back to fall into another.

"You need a night off," our neighbors said. "You can't keep on like this."

They weren't the first people to suggest we needed a break. Hospital staff frequently suggested we stay home for an evening (*We'll take good care of him; you can call as often as you want*), and family and friends begged us to take care of ourselves (*You must be exhausted*). We ignored them all. So why did we let our neighbors take us to the theater?

Because they knew grief and they knew recovery. They had lost a child, and they were still standing. They knew what we needed, not because they'd read it in a self-help book, or because it made sense to their logical brains, but because they had lived it. They had earned the right to give advice.

As we got ready to go out, I felt as though I were onstage myself, playing a role to which I was unaccustomed. It seemed so wrong to even contemplate enjoying ourselves, to put on nice clothes, do my makeup, blow-dry my hair. What were we doing?

I called the hospital. "Is he okay? Are you sure it's all right not to be there tonight?" I worried they'd judge us or think we didn't care. I worried we'd see someone we knew at the theater and they'd think us heartless. I felt so guilty I almost canceled, and only the kindness of our neighbors stopped me. There were almost certainly people they could have invited who would have been better company than this ashen-faced couple who drifted from conversations every few minutes to stare into an abyss of grief. They chose us. They knew what we needed better than we knew ourselves.

By unspoken agreement, we didn't mention hospitals or children as we walked to the theater. The foyer was packed, and I felt suddenly terrified, as though I'd spent years in an underground bunker, far away from people. I held my husband's hand tightly, and our neighbors guided us gently to our seats.

I can't tell you what the pantomime was, or if it was good, but I can tell you that I laughed, which was an odd sensation. The exclamation itself was rusty from misuse, and it prompted a wave of contrition: an incongruous pairing that would become all too familiar over the coming months. I suspect you, too, have felt it.

At its most simplistic level, we feel bad when we feel good.

But listen: We feel bad enough when we feel bad, right? So on the rare occasions when despair lifts and we feel a glimmer of happiness, don't you think we should embrace it? Let ourselves, just for a moment, feel the warmth of the sun on our skin before the clouds move in again?

I have said elsewhere in this book that we have to give in to our emotions—sadness, anger, tearfulness—and this is equally true of happiness. Don't analyze it, don't try to measure or justify it. Just feel it. It's okay to not be okay, but it's just as okay to feel good.

10

I promise you won't always feel so tired

My office was on the third floor of a busy city-center police station. It was functional and bland, the way you might imagine a police inspector's office to be, with a large corner desk, a cupboard in which I hid cereal and tea bags, and two armchairs for when conversations with colleagues were likely to be lengthy. I sat in one of them now, a notebook on my lap, waiting for one of my team to arrive. It was April—a month of appraisals and end-of-year budgets—and through the window I could see the tops of the trees bursting into leaf. Beneath them, a constant hum of activity came from the backyard of the station. The door clunked open and shut, car doors slammed. Sirens were tested at the start of a shift, blue lights sweeping the walls. Snatches of conversations drifted through my open window.

I closed my eyes.

I worked full time and I had three children under two. Nursery fees were prohibitively expensive, so we'd hired a nanny. The second she pulled up outside, I'd leave the house, shouting apologies as I climbed into my own car. "They've had breakfast, but they're not dressed, sorry. Bead-up-the-nose incident. Would you mind unloading the dishwasher? Thank you so much, I'm so sorry, thank you…"

I was pathetically grateful to be allowed to go to work, to reclaim some part of my identity. The events of the previous two years had left me so uncertain, I hardly recognized myself in the mirror. My return to work came with a degree of imposter syndrome I've never felt before or since, but it was nevertheless a relief to be back. Here was a job I (mostly) knew how to do. A job I was (mostly) good at. On the drive into Oxford, I'd button my epaulettes, clip on my tie, and pray for a space at the park & ride, where I'd make a start on my emails as I waited for the bus. By the time I reached my desk at eight o'clock, my metamorphosis from mum to ma'am complete, I felt as though I'd done a full day's work.

"Um…boss?"

I jerked upright and surreptitiously wiped my mouth, from which I suspected a line of drool was trailing. "Yes! Hi! Sorry about that. Right. Ready." I had never felt less ready.

"Tired?"

"Guess so. Ha! Right, let's get down to it." I snapped open my notebook.

There were layers to my tiredness. On the surface sat the sort of tiredness it was acceptable to have in the workplace. The in-early-to-brief-the-response-team or at-my-desk-late-again sort of tiredness. Policing was 24/7, and in addition to my day job, I was now a public order commander, dealing with the sorts of protests and disorder that don't confine themselves to office hours. It was understandable (even, I felt at times, expected) that I was a little tired.

Beneath that was the worn-out fatigue familiar to all parents or carers. Not only the sleepless nights but the mental gymnastics of juggling childcare; the constant fear that someone will fall ill; the worry over school choices and playground bullying; the relentless decisions over what to cook for dinner.

"Kids not sleeping?" the police constable said.

I gave a wry smile. "You know what it's like. Now, how are you finding the new role?"

My children slept reliably well. Out like a light at seven o'clock and not a peep out of them for twelve hours. My own sleeping pattern was a different matter entirely.

The third layer of my tiredness wouldn't be solved with a good night's sleep or a week off work—in fact, I felt more exhausted away from the distractions of work. I was tired because I lay awake fighting guilt and fear; because I read late into the night, afraid to turn off the light. I was tired because when I did sleep, it was as though I were drugged, something dragging me down till I felt as if I were drowning. I would wake in a thick fog, like coming round from anesthetic. I was tired because I was grieving.

Grief fatigue seeps into the very marrow of our bones, weighing us down, so even holding up our head is an effort too far. It makes us ignore our thirst, because getting up to fetch a glass of water is beyond our capabilities. We could sleep for twenty-four hours and still not feel refreshed, because we're not just tired. We're grieving.

The worst of it is that tiredness exacerbates other symptoms of grief—such as anxiety, depression, confusion... And so the cycle continues.

But I don't need to tell you that. You know.

———

Like all elements of grief, the impact it has on sleep will vary from person to person and from one month to another. In the immediate aftermath of Alex's death, I slept as though my body hoped it wouldn't wake up. Sleep felt ever-present, grudgingly allowing me to perform brief, basic functions, before dragging me back into its cloying embrace. I woke exhausted, as though it were already bedtime.

The staff in intensive care, themselves working long and erratic hours, must have been used to parents nodding off next to their babies' incubators. I woke up once to discover someone had draped a blanket around me and tucked my coat beneath my head as it lolled against the chair.

When we eventually made it home from the hospital, with our tiny four-month-old son, I was grateful for the age-old advice to sleep when the baby slept. I willingly sank into the oblivion of sleep, the line blurred between the tiredness of grief and that of the new mother.

If your grief makes you need to sleep all the time, I think that's okay. If you need to curl up on the sofa six times a day, I see no reason why you shouldn't. Bereavement is a trauma. If we were recovering from a dreadful accident—bruised and battered and barely alive—no one would think twice if we slept all night and half the day. Sleep is good. Sleep is healing.

———

Sometimes the reality of bereavement doesn't kick in for a while, and when it does, the symptoms of our grief can change. Several months after Alex's death—when outwardly I seemed to be functioning normally—I stopped sleeping.

I remember a moment about six months after my wedding, when the fact that I was married finally sank in. There had been the excitement of all the preparation, and then the day itself. A honeymoon, gifts to open, thank-you notes to write. Much later, when everyone who was interested had seen the photos, and we had arranged all our lovely presents and visited friends and relatives, it was just the two of us. It was lovely, but it felt strangely flat: a new status quo to which I hadn't yet adjusted.

It was a very different kind of moment after Alex died, but nevertheless, I recognized it. The fight-or-flight adrenaline had dissipated, and the rush of concern had tailed away. There were no more lasagnas on the doorstep, no more cards through the door. It was just us and our grief, and it would be that way forever.

I remember feeling such despair back then, and if this speaks to you at all, I need you to know that I was wrong. In my mixed-up head, I'd made so much progress (I wasn't screwed into a sobbing mess on the floor 24/7, ergo I must have improved) that I imagined my recovery curve had leveled off. This was it. As good as it was going to get. I lay awake at night, staring into the darkness, grieving as much for my old life as for my son. I must have slept, because I had nightmares, but that isn't what I remember from those months. What I remember is being awake, silently sobbing in the near-darkness, feeling as though my heart were breaking.

I dreaded my husband's night shifts. I would send messages at four in the morning: messages that said nothing yet said everything. A blue heart, a string of kisses, a photograph of our boys.

"Are you okay?" he'd ask from his police car somewhere in Oxfordshire.

"I'm fine," I'd tell him. Because what could he do?

What could anyone do?

As time passed, my nighttime sobbing stopped—the way acute pain from an injury settles to a dull ache—but by then, I had lost the habit of sleeping well. By the time my eldest was six, and the twins five, I had learned to function on just a few hours' sleep. I don't know if my performance suffered at work, but I knew it was suffering at home. I had always been ambitious, but I realized that what I'd taken for "having it all" was simply "doing it all." And not always very well.

I quit the police.

It felt like a second bereavement, and I sobbed as I cut up my warrant card. There are many dictionary definitions of grief, but most include death only as an adjunct. *Very deep sadness*, reads the Cambridge English Dictionary, *especially at the death of someone*. Other dictionaries refer to *emotion felt as a result of loss or regret*. The breakup of a relationship, the ending of a friendship, a redundancy, the end of a career… these are all catalysts for grief.

Away from the police, I continued to use work as an excuse not to sleep, spending long evenings writing my debut novel or hustling for freelance work. With my husband working nights, and the children asleep, there was no one to encourage me into a healthier pattern. I stayed at my desk, or downstairs in front of the television, until my head was heavy, and then I stayed some more. I read till my eyes stung with grit and the words swam on the page, not because I wanted to know how the story unfolded, but because exhaustion was the only way I knew to sleep.

During the day, when my mind was busy, there was no room for intrusive thoughts, but nighttime was another matter entirely. I was terrified of silence. Space. Not that I realized at the time what I was avoiding. Rather, I saw sleep as an irritating, necessary evil: something to endure rather than enjoy.

"It's such a waste of time," I sighed. I'd taken the children down to Devon to stay with a writer friend. The twins were perhaps six or seven then, and I was deep into my second crime novel. "Imagine how much I could get done if I didn't have to sleep."

My friend, who loves nothing more than an early night with a pile of cookery books and the promise of eight glorious hours asleep, tutted. "You're looking at it all wrong. Sleep is the *reason* we get things done. It's when our brains make sense of things, how we work things out."

I rejected her logic and continued to burn the candle at

both ends, rarely sleeping before one or two in the morning, chasing away the difficult thoughts with noise and busyness. I dreaded bedtime the way some people dread Monday morning or the end of the tax year, putting it off until I physically couldn't stay awake any longer.

When I woke in the night, I'd reach for my phone, fizzing away any last chance of sleep with status updates, likes, and shares, slotting other people's bite-sized news into every last corner of my mind. By morning, I was wrecked, but it was fine. I had caffeine. I had sugar.

———

Acclimating to being exhausted is not the same as functioning well. Tiredness impacts on your mood, your productivity, your ability to process thoughts and make decisions. I could feel myself slipping, grief and fatigue meshing all too often with apathy, until I couldn't be certain if I was sad, tired, or simply couldn't be bothered.

One January, I made a resolution to leave my phone downstairs at night. It's the only New Year's resolution I have ever kept, and it isn't overstating things to say that it was transformational. Now, when I woke in the night, I had to confront my own thoughts instead of filling my mind with other people's. I realized that for years I'd been trying to drown out what was in my head, when instead I should have been listening to it, allowing my grief to take shape, recognizing and acknowledging it…then letting it pass.

Like most things, this is hard to do when you are recently bereaved. Even now, when I'm in a dark place I prefer to turn on the radio or listen to an audiobook when I go to bed rather than allow my inner voice to take over. In the worst weeks of my grief-fueled insomnia, I became addicted to the low, continuous chatter of the shopping channels. I never bought a single thing, but I will always be grateful for the company of those smiling presenters, whose smooth segues from product to product filled the space where grief waited to pounce.

———

It is Saturday night and my bed is calling to me. It's still early, and there's plenty on TV, but my husband is away and I can almost feel the hug of my duvet and the softness of my pillow beneath my head. I have made some changes—just small ones: new bedding, a scented candle, baskets for the clutter—and my bedroom is a refuge from the house, where the teenagers divest themselves of socks on the stairs and drop crumbs in a trail from kitchen to sofa.

"Will you let the dogs out?" I ask the oldest teen. "And turn off all the lights?"

"Are you going to bed?" He is incredulous. His optimum

waking time is between midday and midnight; he is still young enough to view early bedtimes as a punishment, not a treat.

"I am indeed." I take a cup of herbal tea with me and collect something to read from my study, where the pile of unread books grows steadily taller. I sit briefly at my desk, where I write my nightly list of tomorrow's tasks. If I don't write this list, it will write itself in my head the moment I close my eyes, reminding me how much there is to do, how overwhelming life is.

In bed, I read for half an hour or so. Downstairs, the teens begin to raid the kitchen cupboards, searching for whatever it is they think magically appears after sundown. I slide into the depths of my duvet. It is gloriously comfortable—decadently so—and I feel the blissful woolliness that marks the transition from wakefulness to sleep.

When I wake, I know instinctively that it isn't morning. There is a thickness about the dark; a chill in the air. There's something else, too: a sound from one of the children's rooms on the top floor. Quietly, I slip out of bed and climb the winding staircase to find a sliver of light beneath one of the doors. I push it open. "Can't sleep?"

Tear-stained cheeks shine in the half-light.

"Want to talk?"

A shake of the head. "It's just…"

The sentence disappears. I sit on the bed and offer a shoulder, and we sit in gentle silence. I think of how dark those nights were after Alex died, how long it was before I could switch off the light. I think of how sobs turned me inside out, and how I thought they would never cease.

It's just…

It's just everything, isn't it, when it's dark? It's the silence in the room, pressing against the noise in our heads. It's the *what if*s and the *what now?* The *if only*s and the *why*s. Worries that seem reasonable—even laughable—in daylight swell in the dead of night, when the house is quiet and there is no one around to divide them into more achievable steps, to make plans and offer comforting hugs. Sleep becomes impossible.

Sometimes there is no solution. We can't change decisions made years ago, or take a different path. We can't bring back the people we loved. We have to let our hearts cry and accept that it hurts. We have to believe that it really is darkest before the dawn, and that soon the skies will be streaked with reds and golds and the ache in our chest will subside.

———

As time passes, and your grief eases, sleep will settle into a more practical and predictable pattern. Until then, accept that tiredness is a common symptom of grief. Listen to it. Take that two-hour nap. Sleep when your body wants to sleep. Acknowledge that your routine might be erratic, and that even when you do sleep, you might feel as though you haven't.

Convention tells us to sleep when the sun does, but there are no rules to grief, and if you sleep more soundly in the afternoon, then curl up in the warmth of the sun. If the nights are hard because they're dark and quiet, see what happens if you keep the lights and radio on. Stay with a friend until the worst has passed or watch box sets on repeat till you can quote every line.

The early stages of grief are about survival. We pick a path through the shelled-out remains of our life, and it takes time to find our way home again.

11

I promise you'll find someone who understands

In all the years that have passed since Alex died, my loneliest moments have been when I've been surrounded by people. It's then that I've felt the starkest contrast between other people's lives and mine, when I've felt the pressure of keeping my grief inside because it isn't the right time, because they wouldn't understand.

When Alex's twin brother was three, we held a party. We hired a hall and played games, laid out a table with sandwiches and cake. It wasn't the first birthday party he'd had, but it was the first where I noticed a shift. There were friends invited who hadn't known us when Alex had died—who knew our loss as an anecdote, not an experience lived by proxy—and so it didn't cross their minds that I might find the day hard.

I played with the children and handed out balloons, all

the time feeling as though I were on the sidelines, watching someone else's life. I wanted to mourn my baby on the day I gave birth to him. I wanted to look at photographs and touch the lock of his hair. I wanted to remember the smell of him, the weight of him in my arms. I wanted to cry.

Instead, I had baked a cake and wrapped presents. Now I was lighting candles and singing "Happy Birthday" with a fierce smile on my face, determined to give my son the best birthday he could have. I was making the day about him, just as he deserved, and everyone at the party was doing the same.

Inside, I was breaking.

As our guests were leaving with their tired, chocolatey children, one gave me a hug. "A bittersweet day, I imagine," she said. "But at least you have his brother."

If only she had stopped at the bittersweet. People have a peculiar compulsion to mitigate the terrible with something uplifting, and despite their best intentions, they so often get it wrong. It is easier, I suppose, to apply a *there, there* plaster than it is to sit down and say, *A terrible thing has happened to you. How do you feel? What can I do to make this less awful?*

The bus is late, but at least it's not raining.

Your son died, but at least you have another.

"Thank God!" I wanted to say, flinging up my arms in a hallelujah. "I have three, so that gives me a couple of spares in case I'm careless enough to lose one again. Phew!"

I didn't, of course. I said, *Yes, I'm very lucky*, and I am, I am lucky, but having other children does not make it easier to lose one, just as having two parents doesn't make it okay when one dies. Throughout our lives we love many people, and the loss of each one is its own devastation.

I added a tally mark to the list of clichés I kept at the back of my diary, which felt like a more socially acceptable response than screaming. Pencil tight in my fist, lead splintering against the page; a score for every well-meaning platitude bearer.

In a way, it must be easier that he was so young.

At least he's no longer in pain.

Gone to a better place.

Bingo. Bingo. Bingo.

The bold ones dared to suggest that it might have been *for the best*, as though they'd had an insight into my son's future and considered it a less attractive prospect than death. They said, *It could have been worse* and *Life goes on* and *There's no sense in dwelling on what might have been.* Whatever condolence dictionary people were consulting needed rewriting. Time and time again I heard that Alex's *suffering has ended*, that *everything happens for a reason*, and that *what doesn't kill us makes us stronger.*

Full house.

Many of these platitudes aren't just hurtful, they're wrong.

Our loved ones haven't *gone to a better place*; the best place was here, by our side, and if the world wasn't a happy place for them, then the world should have changed. Of course we didn't want our babies, our parents, our siblings, our friends to suffer. But neither did we want them to die.

———

Platitudes have cost me friendships. There has been no dramatic parting of ways, but grief—and the way others react to it—can make us feel differently about people. Life is too short, we realize, to spend it with those who don't make us feel good, or who minimize our pain in order to relieve their own discomfort.

"Come on now," one of my friends used to say whenever I was falling. "Let's talk about something less depressing."

Well, that would be nice, wouldn't it? To switch off our heads so we aren't crying inside, even when we're smiling. To erase the sadness from our hearts and replace it with kittens and unicorns. That's not our reality. Our reality is a pain that will be with us forever. Grief is a chronic debilitating illness, with symptoms that come and go. It can't be cured, only managed.

When people try to change the subject, it's rarely a genuine attempt to cheer us up; it's because grief is uncomfortable to talk about. Tedious for some. Unpleasant for many. But that isn't our problem—it's theirs. Do they think we *like* feeling this way? We'd give anything to be free from grief. We'd love to have not lost our loved ones or (because death is unavoidable) to have made peace with our loss so we were no longer consumed by pain and guilt and longing. It is uncomfortable for us, too. It is unpleasant for us, too. And is there anything more tedious than to live a life so flat, so sad, so grief-stricken? Other people's discomfort is nothing compared to ours.

But we *need* to talk about our experiences. Talking about our emotions helps us to process them; talking about our loved ones helps to keep them alive in our hearts.

"Find a good counselor," the consultant advised after Alex died, and so I diligently found one with two leather chairs in the center of her office. They were positioned at a slight angle to each other, presumably to make the situation feel less confrontational, but I still felt uncomfortable. The therapist left long pauses after each of my answers, waiting for me to fill the silence. It's an old trick (one I used numerous times in police suspect interviews), and recognizing it made it feel patronizing. I let the pauses stretch until she had no choice but to ask another question. I felt instinctively that she didn't—couldn't—understand, so I clung on to my thoughts and emotions, as though giving them up would be accepting defeat. The counselor's questions felt like challenges rather than invitations, and instead of opening up, I shut down. I suspect she was as relieved as I was when I ended the relationship after three sessions.

Counseling was a waste of time and money, I concluded. I was not surprised by this outcome: the early stages of grief feel so permanent, it's impossible to envisage a time when we won't be crushed by it. How could talking help? How could anything help?

"Have you tried Pilates?" asked one friend when I mentioned I was finding things hard. *I just keep crying*, I'd said. *All the time. For no reason at all.* She had already suggested enrolling in a cookery course and volunteering for a helpline, and had sent me several articles on grief. She was a Fixer. There are times when Fixers are useful, but I couldn't be fixed. Not then. What I needed was a Listener. An Acknowledger. Someone who would hear my words and hold them for a time, recognizing their importance, their validity. Someone who wouldn't try to analyze or contradict, offer advice or suggest solutions. The best friends are those who ask what they can do to help, just as they might if you suffered from chronic physical pain. *You need your wheelchair today? My arm? I'm here for you.*

My Fixer friend wasn't a bad friend, she was just the wrong sort of friend at that moment in my grief. Likewise, although I hadn't seen it at the time, there had likely been nothing wrong with the counselor I saw, but she'd been a bad fit for me at that particular time. I hadn't been ready to be fixed.

———

When we talk about a journey through grief, it's important to remember that we don't all travel the same path or move at the same pace. You may have loved your mother as deeply as your sister did, but your grief is as unique to you as your love for her was. Not more, not less, just different, and you and your sibling will need different types of support. Try not to compare your own grief—or your recovery—to anyone else's.

It's human nature to seek parallels for experience, our inbuilt alternative to computer algorithms that predict *if you liked that, you'll like this...*

You enjoyed your holiday in Portugal? Oh, you must try Croatia! You'll love it.

You've had shingles? You poor thing—I had that once and I was hospitalized.

It is never okay to do this with grief.

No one knows how you feel except for you. You own your experience, your grief, even if the person you loved was loved by others, too. If five people were to be dropped in the middle of the ocean, they would not all fare the same. One would be a stronger swimmer; another would cope better with icy temperatures. One would panic; one might swim well for a time and then tire. Each would have a different relationship with the water, a different reaction to the crisis. I'm sharing my own path through grief in the hope that parts of it will be familiar to you, and that you'll find comfort in knowing there's an end to the awfulness of early grief.

But I don't know how you feel.

———

After Alex died, I tried to go to a support group hosted by a local church. Groups can be an incredibly valuable resource for some people, and if they help you, I'm truly glad. If they're not for you, you're not alone. I found the collective outpouring of grief overwhelming, leaving me feeling as though I'd been crushed by falling rocks. Like with the counselor, like with the Fixer friend, it might simply have been the wrong time—or the wrong group—but I didn't feel able to handle so many stories of loss. Instead, I found support in one-to-one conversations with people who were living with grief. In particular, I was drawn to people who were several years into their journey; people who—I realize as I write this—were where I am now.

I became friendly with a woman from my children's school who had experienced a stillbirth some years before I met her. Sometimes I would call in after the school run, standing at the door wide-eyed with the effort it had taken not to break down in the playground. No reason, just because. You know the way it goes.

"Okay?" she'd say, searching my face. I'd shake my head wordlessly, and it was enough. "I'll put the kettle on."

It's such a relief not to have to explain why we're feeling the way we are, that there's no particular reason why today is harder than any other day. We just woke up this way. Friends who understand grief don't pity us, or gossip about us. They don't tread on eggshells trying not to talk about the person we loved when we're desperate to keep their memory alive. They don't pepper conversations with platitudes, because they've heard them all themselves. They've felt that spark of anger at the suggestion that it was all *for the best*.

———

You might imagine I wouldn't need to find friends to talk to, or even counselors, because who better to talk to than the one person who understood exactly what I was going through. Someone who had lived the same experience, firsthand, and whose grief matched mine in every desperate, agonizing way. My husband.

If I could only give you one piece of advice about grief, it would be this: when you're drowning, the best person to save you is never someone else who's drowning.

"It's like when two people have the flu," said one of the intensive care nurses soon after Alex died. "You can't look after each other when you're both sick."

My husband and I were both so sick, for such a long time.

In the weeks after Alex died, after my husband had cautiously returned to work, I had a rare good day. Nothing extraordinary happened; it was simply a day when I felt a glimmer of hope, the way the clouds shift on a gloomy day, allowing a tiny shaft of light to break through. I felt lighter. Stronger. I took myself to a bookshop, then had coffee. I watched people going about their business, and I didn't long to be them. I was doing okay.

When I got home, my husband was there, and I knew without either of us needing to speak that his own clouds had rolled overhead. I'm almost too ashamed to admit that I wanted to walk back out. I knew that tomorrow—perhaps even in a few hours—I'd be back in the darkness myself, but for now, I could feel the warmth of the sun and I wanted so badly to keep it.

———

Soon after I left the police, I tried counseling again. I was sleeping badly, and my days were punctuated with bouts of crying that left me drained. I was diagnosed with post-traumatic stress disorder and referred to a counselor, whose office was at the top of a narrow staircase. It was light and airy, messier than the first woman's place, but with chairs placed at exactly the same angle. Page one of the counselor's manual, perhaps.

I liked her instantly. I told her everything, and as I did, I realized how much better I was than a few years earlier. How much stronger I was. I cried as I relived the decision we'd made, the final moments with our son, but I could still breathe. I stayed upright. When the counselor asked questions, she didn't bait me with loaded pauses; but then perhaps she didn't need to—I was free with my answers. When the hour was up, I left feeling lighter. The counselor hadn't given me any quick fixes—there are no quick fixes for grief—but I was armed with strategies to handle the sudden bouts of grief that too often caught me unawares. Some of them worked; others didn't. Experts can help us build a toolkit for grief, but we're the only ones who can try each tool out and see what fits.

Many years later, I was talking to my sister about what I'd come to think of as my hinterland: the years when I'd felt cut off from the world.

"I was so lonely," I said. "Everyone just stopped calling. No one asked if we were okay."

"We tried." Her face was creased with sadness. "We kept trying, but you wouldn't let us in."

It's true.

I didn't know it at the time, but I look back now and I can remember the times when family asked how I was doing and I said I was okay, when friends suggested they come over and I said I was busy. Grief made me lonely, but I think I might have made myself lonelier.

———

When life becomes a little overwhelming, and the past threatens to interrupt the peace of the present, I go for a walk. I was on such a walk when I saw a tree stretching right across the path. If you walk through the woodland around Chipping Norton, you might even see it yourself. This tree must have fallen many, many years ago: the ground is settled, and the earth has built up again around the base.

If it had been alone in the middle of a field when it toppled, it would have crashed to the ground and died. But this tree grew in a forest. It stood surrounded by other trees—some smaller, some larger—and when it fell, all those years ago, it was caught by these other trees. Its roots were wrenched from the ground: nerve endings exposed and vulnerable, brittle and dead. But just enough of them still reach into the earth to keep it alive. It rests in the arms of others, who have silently kept it from falling to the ground. They have saved it. They continue to save it.

The slant of this huge trunk is absurd. It lurches across the path like a drunkard bent on self-destruction. Surely a tree cannot grow at such an angle? But slowly, carefully, over months and years, the branches learned to adapt. They changed their path, twisted upward, and pushed their way toward the sky.

And so the tree grows. It makes no pretense at normality: it leans upon others, and it finds a way to live, and to breathe, and to grow.

This is what our supporters do. We don't always find them straight away, and they're not always in the place we think they should be. But I promise they're out there. We might find them in family, in village hall groups, or therapists' offices. They might be old friends or virtual strangers. Their support might be quiet or vocal, practical, or emotional. We might find them right away, while we're still standing, or when we begin to fall.

Either way, they're here to catch us, if we let them.

12

I promise you won't always be winded by someone else's happiness

Toward the end of my police career, I had an office in a busy station. It was a few minutes' walk from there to the canteen, and the route I took made it even longer. It ate precious minutes from an already busy day, but it meant I didn't have to walk past the Photograph.

One day I was heading for a coffee with a colleague, and it would have been strange to have suggested walking a longer route. The Photograph was shot in a bright, white studio, as they all seemed to be back then. Eight by six, in an inexpensive frame, it stood on a desk, lording it over piles of paperwork and mugs of half-drunk tea. In it, two parents lay on the floor. Children are piled on top of them, heads thrown back in laughter. Blue jeans, bare feet, crisp white T-shirts. Joy pouring from every pixel.

They taunted me, the family in that photo. They locked

eyes with me, gleeful in their happiness, their together-
ness. I hated them. I hated the parents, the tween, the
toddler. I hated the baby. I hated their happiness, their
no-cares-in-the-world, their matching outfits. I imagined
their lives to be one long over-saturated photograph; that
they lived forever in their blue jeans and spotless shirts,
always laughing, always joking. Not for them the sharp
stab of grief when they posed for a photograph; the empty
arm around a missing child. Not for them the under-
current of guilt beneath fleeting moments of happiness,
because grief is a thief who robs even those moments of
their purity.

As we drew level with the desk, I stared at the photo.
It seemed to be displayed just for me, flaunted at just the
right angle. Why did people have photos of their families
on their desks, anyway? Were they so absent-minded they
needed visual reminders? It was showboating, that was all.
*My family's better than your family. Look how happy my kids
are. Look how alive they are.*

The owner of the desk was looking at me curiously. I
knew him only enough to exchange a greeting in passing.
Certainly not well enough to be scrutinizing the occupants
of a photo frame as though it were a spot-the-difference quiz.

"Lovely photo," I managed. I bit the inside of my cheek
until my mouth filled with metal.

––––

There are moments in grief I have found to be mercifully brief. Others are insidious and deep-rooted; the bindweed from which your garden is never quite free, no matter how often you pull it up. Bitterness was my bindweed. I felt it physically: a hot, angry surge. My skin tightened, as though it could barely contain what was inside, as though I might split open and my sourness would flood out.

I didn't wish anyone ill, but at the same time, I didn't wish them well. My resentment had no boundaries and, seemingly, no logic. I had lost a child, so it was unsurprising that pregnancy and birth announcements were hard to deal with, but (ever the over-achiever) I was bitter, too, at every wedding, every graduation, every new job or house move. I placed the happiness of other people in inverse proportion to my own wretchedness, and some days my mental state depended entirely on how often I saw someone laugh. I could only hold it together if other people were struggling, too, if they were as unhappy as I was.

I can't tell you if this is normal—I'm not an expert, and this is not that kind of book—but I can tell you it was normal for me, for a long time. It isn't the sort of conversation one easily has with friends (*Hey, you know when you got that promotion? I smashed a plate and pretended it was you, ha ha*), so it is dangerously easy to imagine I was the only one who felt this way. Experience, though, has taught me that we are never as unique as we think we are, so if you recognize yourself on this page, I think we should both claim it as normal.

It won't surprise you to know that social media was not my friend during this time. Facebook is a relentless torrent of smugness, with its galleries of joyful moments and happy families. Automated prompts nudge us to publicly celebrate Mothering Sunday, Valentine's Day, Father's Day. It is a platform built to share happiness, and each time I logged on, it tipped me further down into grief.

Great pics! I'd post. *Looks like a fab day!* The exclamation marks, always the exclamation marks, their chirpy enthusiasm compensating for my bitterness. They *were* great pictures, it *did* look like a fabulous day, and I was glad—I really was—that my friends' lives were so perfect. But deep down, where it really mattered, something shattered.

———

I suspect it is easier to be an unpleasant person if you have no idea that you are unpleasant. There are people who go through life scattering bitterness without any recognition that their words are laced with bile, and they don't wrestle with their conscience over it because being horrible is such a natural state for them that they don't even consider it to be horrible.

But I knew. I was rotting from the inside, and I knew it. If you experience this, you'll know it, too. You'll scroll through photographs of a friend's happy day (or, if you're like me, you'll seek out the social media feeds of happy strangers in order to torture yourself still further), and you'll feel the canker eat away at your soul.

It is an awful way to live, and I stayed that way for longer than anyone who knew me will imagine. A sour, envious, unpleasant person. I hated other people's happiness, but I hated myself more. Grief had awakened a bitterness I didn't know I was capable of, and I had no idea how to rid myself of it.

———

Like many facets of my grief, coming to terms with other people's good fortune has happened in several stages. For a long time, my bitterness was indiscriminate. I felt the gut punch of someone else's achievements regardless of how they related to my own life. A friend's tennis success felt like a personal attack, despite having no inclination to learn myself; two friends laughing in a café sent a current of loneliness through me, even though I'd chosen to be by myself that day. I had found a publisher for my debut novel—something I'd dreamed of since I was a child—yet I couldn't shake this sense of envy for other people's happiness. I had to mute one police acquaintance on social media when she was celebrating her promotion to a new rank, because I was eaten up with bitterness. I had chosen to leave the force, so why did I resent someone who had stayed? Because they had made it work, and I hadn't?

It might seem obvious that one person's dream holiday bears no relation to another person's grief, but in my experience it's a difficult lesson to learn. Humans are hardwired for fairness, and when someone you love dies, the world tilts. Why us? Why *only* us? Why should others fly when we are falling?

I did what I always do, which is to pretend everything is okay.

There are lots of things wrong with this approach, especially if it leads—as it has done for me, at times—to bottling everything up so badly you break, but as a fundamental principle there's something to be said for faking it. In the workplace, we're told to *dress for the job you want*, because of the psychological benefits to both the interviewee and their assessor. In a similar vein, *be the person you want to be* has not only kept me (relatively) sane, it has slowly dissolved my bitterness.

Every day, I made myself say something nice. I congratulated friends on their career success, their holiday of a lifetime, and—yes—even their tennis scores. I smiled at babies, at laughing friends, at families enjoying the sunshine. Slowly, the disconnect between my words and what I felt inside began to close. I began to mean what I said.

———

I look back sometimes at my early days on social media, when the children were babies. I posted hundreds of photographs. They've appeared on the feeds of people I know well, and less well, harvesting the hearts and comments I like to pretend don't matter. Only I know the true story behind the filters; only I can remember how I was reeling with grief, anxiety, and depression. I look at a photo taken at the wildlife park, when my chest felt so tight I had to grip the side of the penguin enclosure to stay upright; a picture posted from a party where we lined up the kids in height order, and all I could see was the boy who wasn't there. I scroll through a decade of birthdays and Christmas celebrations, of nights out with the girls, when all I wanted to do was crawl home and cry.

In every photograph, I'm smiling.

So much can be hidden by a smile. It's easy to forget, when you're gripped by grief, that nobody's life is perfect. No one's life is filled with laughter from start to finish, no one's days are untouched by sorrow, or worry, or fear. We take photographs at happy moments in our lives because we need to preserve them; because we know we'll need to return to them on days when we can't raise a smile. The joy we paste on our faces for a photograph represents how we *want* to feel—how we want to *remember* we felt—not how we truly feel.

When someone's happiness takes your breath away for all the wrong reasons, remind yourself that you're seeing a single page in their life, not the whole story. A picture paints a thousand words, but there are many ways to read them.

———

You are not a terrible person. The bitterness you're feeling isn't the real you. It's a veneer applied by grief, and it will slowly wear away until it vanishes altogether. Your friends will keep sharing their good news, and you'll keep saying through gritted teeth how pleased you are, and how great it is, and all the time your insides will hollow out with pain. And then, one day, you'll realize your fingers aren't curled into bitter fists, your nails are no longer carving distress signals in your palm. You'll realize that when you heard your friend's news, your first thought was not of what you'd lost, but of what they had gained.

Every person you've ever met could find happiness, and it wouldn't lessen your chances of doing the same.

You know that, right?

They could be mired in grief, and it still wouldn't take away yours.

Happiness isn't a zero-sum game; it doesn't depend on other people's good fortune.

When someone dies, it isn't only that other people's joy is hard to hear about, it's that we can't counter it with anything joyful of our own. The small pleasures we might have found in our old lives seem meaningless when set against the backdrop of our grief. So the cherry tree is full of blossoms. Big deal. It's just a tree. Due a week off work? What's to celebrate, when all that means is more empty time to fill with sadness?

You know what I'm going to say, don't you?

It gets easier.

There *will* be good news again—something that fills your heart with joy. I promise. It won't feel the way it did before you broke, but not for the reasons you think.

The difference will be in the way you choose to share your news.

You'll hesitate before picking up the phone or posting online. You'll wonder whether it's the right time, whether you've chosen the right person to tell. What's going on in their life? Can your news wait?

Loss breeds bitterness, but it creates compassion, too, and when one has burned itself out, the other will remain. Grief doesn't turn you into a terrible person; it makes you a kind one.

———

Despite my best intentions, I have never quite managed to kick my social media habit. I justify my presence across numerous platforms on the basis that I need it for work, that it's nice to stay in touch with far-flung friends. I scroll through my timeline over a morning cup of tea, looking at holiday snaps and widening my eyes at posts that reveal a seemingly pleasant new acquaintance to be a raging fascist. *Unfriend.*

A friend is celebrating the birth of a new arrival. I have reached that stage where—although my own children are thankfully not yet ready to procreate—my friends are having grandchildren, and this new baby is the first of a generation. She is wrinkled and pink; nestled in the arms of her mother, who reclines in an inflatable birthing pool, exhausted and elated. It was a home birth, I read, over in a few short hours. A calming midwife, essential oils, music playing. A beautiful experience, the post says. I think briefly of my own traumatic labors—the urgency, the crowded rooms, the flicker of ceiling lights as doctors raced my trolley into surgery—but there is no connection between the two. I write a message— *She's beautiful—congratulations! So glad they had the birth they'd hoped for*—and I mean it.

I switch to Twitter for a final fix before I finish my tea. Here, my timeline is less personal and more business—writers and editors, readers and critics. An author I know well has won a prize; a prize for which I was not even considered, let alone shortlisted. I read her excited post and wait for the flash of envy that was once ever present.

I realize I'm frowning.

Here it comes. Like an old friend.

Look, I never said I was perfect...

13

I promise you won't always be broken by anniversaries

The buildup to that first anniversary, on 10 December, began in September. As the autumn leaves fell, I felt as though any progress I had made over the intervening months had been reversed. Here I was, right where I'd started: in abject despair. By Guy Fawkes Day—the twins' birthday—I didn't want to leave the house. The anniversary loomed in front of me, as solid and oppressive as a mountain range I had no hope of crossing.

On the day itself, we visited Alex's grave. I was six months pregnant and a mess of hormones. In retrospect, it was the wrong thing to do—I found it traumatic rather than comforting—but I think it can take a while to figure out how we want to spend these significant days. I was glad when it was over, and woke the next day with a huge sense of relief.

That pattern—building dread throughout the autumn,

relief once 10 December was over—continued for a number of years. I always took the anniversary itself off work. It was protection for others as much as for myself, knowing that the slightest thing might tip me over the edge. I worried I would respond to an accidentally ill-judged comment with tears or anger, or with a far worse comment of my own.

I wished I could take even longer off work: from 5 November to 10 December. They felt like limbo, those five weeks between Alex's birth date and the day he died; the way we'd lived a kind of limbo when he'd been alive. *This time four years ago*, I'd think, *he was alive.* I would be unable to rest, as though—if I tried hard enough—I might be able to stop what came afterward. Every year, I would be able to hold it together until 5 November. The date was not only Alex's birthday but, of course, his twin's, and nothing could be allowed to cast a shadow over his celebrations. The specter would not visit this feast.

Afterward, though.

Once the wrapping paper was discarded, the candles blown out, the cake enjoyed... *Now*, I thought. *Those precious five weeks start now.*

The ensuing days were unbearable. Throughout the rest of the year, the gaps between bad days had grown considerably longer over time, until grief was no longer the backdrop to my days but a curtain, drawn mostly to the side. But for the five weeks between 5 November and 10 December, grief wrapped itself around me with all the intensity of those early days. I planned nothing, knowing I would be unable to see people, that I would simply be willing away each day, desperate to get to 11 December. There was no logic to my dread of those weeks; but then, grief is often illogical.

There are many people in my life who remember the date of Alex's death. Fewer now, perhaps, than in the beginning, but that is to be expected. The ripples grow smaller the further out they are from the stone. Nevertheless, on 10 December each year, I receive messages.

Thinking of you.

Love you.

Hope you're doing okay.

One friend, who never knew Alex, but who knows only too well the pain of losing a child, sends a text message every year without fail. I hope they know how much it means to me.

———

Five years after Alex had died, I caught myself, mid-November, and realized something extraordinary. I felt all right. Neither tearful nor depressed; not angry or despairing. Just...normal. *I've beaten it*, I thought, which should have been the first alarm bell. Grief isn't something we can fight. When close friends asked how I was, I said, *I'm doing great!*

"I think I'll be okay this year," I said, referring to the anniversary itself. The anticipation, I knew, was always harder than the day itself.

"Do you want me to take the day off work?" asked my husband.

I smiled. "No, I'll be fine." I felt proud of myself. Relieved the awfulness had passed.

On 10 December, I woke with a leaden sensation in my stomach, like the beginnings of a virus. I took the children to school. I felt distanced from everything, as though I were sitting on the bottom of a swimming pool. By the time I returned home, my breathing had become shallow and fast, and I curled into a ball in the corner of the sitting room, needing to be grounded against as many surfaces as possible. I started crying and couldn't stop, agonizing full-body sobs that made me gasp for air.

Two hours later, I was still there. My eyes had swollen into slits and my nose was so blocked that tissues were pointless. Swallowing made strange clicking noises in my ears. There is nothing glamorous about grief.

How are you doing? A message from a friend. I'd been scrolling through photographs of Alex, berating myself once again for not taking more. Why did I only have one photograph of me holding him? And not a single picture of me with both my boys? Why do we always think we'll have more time?

Okay... I started typing, then stopped. *Not great, actually. Shall I come over?*

I didn't answer. I've never been good at accepting help, and this...this was pathetic, wasn't it? Crying and screaming, years after he'd died, when neither of those things would bring him back or make me better. What use would company be? Nothing my friend could do would help.

She came. She knocked quietly on the door and wrapped me in a hug, pretending not to notice that I smeared her shoulder with my streaked face. She put fresh flowers in a vase and opened an enormous bar of chocolate while I scrubbed my face with cold water and blew my nose again and again.

When the tea had brewed, we sat at the kitchen table. She passed on a juicy piece of gossip, filled me in on what she was doing at work. We ran through the houses for sale in town, and debated whether a bigger kitchen trumped a garage.

We didn't talk about Alex at all.

That's the funny thing about grief: sometimes you need to talk, and sometimes you just need someone to understand. Someone to walk alongside you, waiting for your cue. When I think back over all the 10 Decembers I've had since Alex died, it's these people I think about the most. The friend who gave me a yellow rose to plant so that every year it would bring me comfort. The people who remember alongside the birthday wishes for my growing son to also mark the day for his brother.

———

Those difficult days—the ones we can predict; the ones fixed by the calendar—extend beyond the date your loved one died. They include birthdays and Christmases, wedding anniversaries and dates of first kisses. Every September, I stop looking at social media until the back-to-school photos have finished. No matter that I have three of my own in school uniform; I will always remember the one who didn't live to wear one.

Yes, every September. Even now. I promised you I'd be honest, and although I will tell you time and time again that the years will heal you, every wound leaves a scar. I know now that the autumn no longer heralds a sense of dread, and that Christmas is once again a happy occasion. But I know, too, the dates in the future when I will retreat to a quiet room and cry for my boy. His eighteenth birthday. His twenty-first. The country-wide migration of students to university, toasters and duvets in tow. As I write this—as I think about those milestones—I'm crying in a way I rarely do now. It is all so unfair, isn't it? This pain we learn to carry so well, and for so long: sometimes it has to come out.

Anniversaries are really, really hard. They can be cruel reminders of another year spent grieving, another year we haven't spent with the person we loved so much. They can make us feel as though we're on a train, pulling away from someone we never wanted to leave behind, terrified of the moment that speck in the distance disappears altogether. *I can't believe it's been three years*, people say. *Five years. Seven. Fifteen.* They—and we—have missed so much.

However tough we find anniversaries, I think they're a useful part of our grieving process. There comes a time when we move beyond the acute phase of bereavement and are functioning more normally, but we haven't stopped grieving. Anniversaries allow our grief to break through the surface, releasing some of the tension we might not know we're carrying. They give us permission to focus on our grief and a socially acceptable excuse for feeling sad. We can say to people: *I'm finding this week hard—it would have been Mum's seventieth*, and they know to give us space.

The acute pain of anniversaries will dissipate. You can mark them in the way that feels right to you, and for as long as you need—or want—to mark them. If what you need is to stay indoors and cry—to pore over photos or watch your wedding video on a loop—then that's what you should do. For lots of us, anniversaries are when we feel most connected to our grief, but it's equally okay if you want to gloss over them—to make it just another day.

Over time, each passing anniversary becomes not a marker of how long you've been apart but a measure of how far you've come. How strong you've been.

Some people draw comfort from turning these key moments—be they anniversaries, birthdays, or some other significant date—into something positive. I don't think this can be forced, and you shouldn't put pressure on yourself to celebrate someone's life when you're still struggling to cope with their death, but you might be able to think of small ways to bring color to these difficult days. A friend of mine marks her late parents' wedding anniversary by using their beautiful china tea set; another bakes her husband's favorite cake. You might go for a walk, or light a candle, or take yourself out for lunch. My only word of caution is against creating traditions that can't be sustained. Bringing the whole family together on Dad's birthday is wonderful until someone can't make it and the day becomes a further loss, instead of a celebration.

The year after that awful false start, when I'd thought myself over it (as if we're ever over it), I decided I needed a distraction. Something gentle yet significant; quiet but not silent. My husband would be home from work, but I couldn't bear the thought of going out for lunch, seeing pain in his eyes I knew would mirror mine, searching for conversation, when all either of us wanted to say was *Why? Why did this happen? Why does it still hurt so much?*

"We'll decorate the tree," I announced over breakfast. The shops were crammed with Christmas presents and gaudy decorations; huge signs by the sides of roads urged us to *Order Your Free Range Turkey!* and *Pick Your Own Tree!*

"It's another two weeks till Christmas," my husband said.

His reluctance to put up the tree early was largely my fault, which was, in turn, the legacy of childhood traditions. Festive decorations couldn't go up until 16 December: the day after my younger sister's birthday.

"I'd really like to do it today," I said. "On Alex's day." That was how it was noted in my diary, lest I should somehow forget and schedule something difficult, or emotional, or insultingly mundane. *Alex's day.*

I'd like to tell you we drove into snowy mountains and held hands as we wandered through an alpine forest. That I warmed my hands on hot chocolate as my husband wielded an ax and felled our chosen tree; that my mittens matched my hat, and that we laughed as we tried to tie the tree to the top of our comically small car.

The reality is that we went to the garden center. I think we had an argument (*How big is too big?*). We drove home with the tree squashed into our (too small) car and spent the rest of the day trying to keep it upright and wondering if there would be any needles left on it come Christmas given the number already on the carpet.

That evening, when the children had eaten and were in their pajamas, the curtains drawn against the cold, the five of us decorated the tree. King's College Choir sang the carols my father had always played at Christmas, and I curbed my tendency to perfection in favor of the riot of unbalanced baubles preferred by the small but vocal majority. When every trinket and garland was hung, my husband lifted our biggest child onto his shoulders to place the star on top of the tree.

And of course I thought of Alex, and how he should have been there too, and of course I was sad; but it is impossible not to feel joy when three excitable children are draping tinsel around themselves and *oohing* in wonder at another shiny bauble. How lucky I was to be here to see this day.

Alex's day became Tree Day: a day when the whole family does something together (a rarity, now that we are into the teenage years). Instead of a day to be dreaded, it has become a glorious bright spot in my diary. At odd times of the year, I happen upon a decoration in a gift shop, and as I take it to the till, I feel something more like love than loss.

———

It is December, fifteen years after Alex died. We have not been to the garden center, because an article I read in the

Guardian convinced me that an artificial tree (if used for many years) is more environmentally friendly. Secretly, I hate this perfectly shaped tree. I hope we will drag it from the garage to discover that mice have eaten it, and that we will have to rush out and buy a proper tree, which will lean precariously in the bay window and drop its needles by St. Stephen's Day.

This year's Tree Day is…inconvenient. I am behind on a book, due with my editor that day, and my husband is out in the evening. Two of the children have rugby training at six, and the third will be late home from school.

"We don't have to decorate the tree on Friday," I say. The teenagers are eating breakfast, and I'm leaning against the stove—the only warm place in the house. "We could do it on Saturday."

"S'pose." A shrug from one as she slides off her stool.

"Or do most of it on Thursday." I have always tried not to put pressure on my children to feel a certain way about the death of their brother. Tree Day is important to me, but it doesn't have to be important to them. "Then," I say, thinking out loud, "on Friday, we can put the star—"

"No." This from Alex's twin. Quiet, but adamant. "It has to be Friday."

"Friday it is, then."

I put it in the calendar: a shared event between four and

six o'clock. for any member of the family who wants to be there.

At 3.59 p.m. on Friday, I send my book to my editor and close my laptop. There is a brief argument over what film to have on (*The Boy Called Christmas* wins), and a tussle over whether tinsel is retro cool (me) or still tacky (the kids), then I lay out the decorations and we begin.

It is my favorite Tree Day yet. The teens drift in and out, abandoning the tree for seemingly hilarious exchanges on their phones, before coming back to rearrange my decorations into something more *aesthetic*. My husband has made a saucepan of mulled wine with a dangerous amount of brandy in it, and I sink into the sofa with a glass—the tree half finished—and watch the film. On the coffee table in front of me is a bowl of clove-studded oranges, out of which one of the kids has, inexplicably, picked out an entire row of cloves, lining them up neatly on the edge of the bowl. Clearly their commitment to aesthetics doesn't extend to my bowls of oranges.

The tree is almost done. There are plaintive complaints that it *doesn't feel Christmassy yet*, so I open a box of chocolates, which seems to do the trick.

"Just the star, then," I say, looking at the discarded bubble wrap and boxes of rejected baubles.

"It's my turn."

"No it isn't—you did it last year."

I don't remember when we started taking turns to place the star, and I never remember who did it the previous year, but the children always do. This year it seems it is the turn of our second-born—younger than Alex by a whole twenty minutes—who is far, far too big for his father's shoulders. He stands on a stool and I hug his legs to stop him from falling.

Afterward, when I've tidied away the boxes and the film has finished, he and I admire the tree, with its twinkly lights and (slightly lopsided) star. He is as tall as me now—taller, he says, although I continue to dispute it—and for a second, I feel his brother standing next to us. Fifteen years to the day since Alex died. How did that happen?

"Happy Tree Day," I say. To both my boys.

14

I promise you won't always be shaken by questions you can't answer

"How many kids do you have?"

The question came a long time after my heart had broken; longer still before it would heal. I was standing in the playground, a warm summer breeze blowing my hair in my eyes, and the chatter of children escaping through the classroom windows. I fought the urge to run. I'd already left the question unanswered for too long, and now the woman—a new parent at the school—was looking at me oddly, because who doesn't know how many children they have? Five minutes from now, three children would break away from their classrooms and run to me, spilling feathers and glitter and indoor shoes, and that would be a response, of sorts. But five minutes is a long time to wait for an answer, and the woman tipped her head to one side. She was bemused by my silence, by the way my mouth was working wordlessly.

"How many?" she said again, thinking I'd missed the question. I should have changed the subject while I had the chance—offered an opinion on the new slide, the PTA social, global warming. Instead, she'd said it louder, and now I had to answer, but some questions want an answer that simply can't be found.

I had two children.

One died.

I had two more.

How many did that make? It felt like a macabre riddle, a math question to challenge your heart, not your head. Declaring three children felt like forgetting my firstborn, but claiming four invited confusion, more difficult questions. Both answers felt like lies.

The classroom doors opened, and teaching assistants fed a stream of children to the waiting parents.

"Here are mine!" I said cheerfully, with a smile that didn't fit, crouching down to scoop up the artwork and the book bags and the hugs I would never take for granted.

There was her answer. Three children. Three, where there should be four.

Don't make me say it.

———

There have been times over the last eighteen years when I have been less hesitant with my answers. When I have known it would prompt confusion, or upset the person I was talking to, but nevertheless, I went ahead.

"Technically, four," I've said, my tone clipped. "But one of them died."

It's a cruel way to answer a question offered as conversational appetizer. It turns small talk to big talk without so much as a trigger warning, but why shouldn't we be honest? Why *aren't* we honest?

How was your weekend?

It was great, thanks.

Was it? Or did you spend it packing up your late mother's things? Did you choose a headstone for your wife? Write the eulogy for a friend you'd give anything to see again?

It was tough, we should say. *I'm grieving, and right now I'm finding it really hard.*

If that's difficult for someone to hear, I think we have to ask ourselves whose problem that is. Spoiler: it isn't ours. If we worry too much about how people will respond, we might not say anything at all. If we stay silent, we perpetuate the stigma around death, keeping it behind closed doors when—for the sake of our collective mental health—we should be talking about it as openly as birth.

By not referencing our grief, we might also be underestimating those people who are interested enough in us to ask how we are. I was still with the police when a colleague

I hadn't worked with for long asked if I had plans for the weekend. I told him it was my son's fourth birthday and we were planning to visit a wildlife park.

He smiled. "Sounds like fun."

"Yes," I said, and then I found I was still talking. "It's a tricky day, because he was a twin, you see, only his brother died. I always find it hard."

He didn't miss a beat. "I'm so sorry. Does your son remember him?"

It was something I'd wondered myself. I'd watched him as a baby, curled into a crescent-shaped echo of the ultrasound image I still kept in my purse, and wondered if he felt the absence of his twin. If he knew his rounded form made an apostrophe now, instead of speech marks.

"I don't know," I said.

My colleague was thoughtful. "I expect he does, on some level. Which is nice, don't you think?"

I did. I carried the exchange home with me and felt comforted all weekend, both by its sentiment and by the encounter with someone who hadn't flinched at the mention of death.

People can surprise us.

———

The ease with which I have talked about Alex has ebbed and flowed over the years. The way I talk about him today will be different from how I speak of him tomorrow, because grief is a river that never stops moving and can swell from a trickle to a torrent overnight.

Nowadays I steer conversations so that they don't upset or anger me, and (because I'm kinder now than I was in early grief) so they don't upset other people. A full stop after "My son died" leaves silence into which the wrong words can easily fall, and so I make the line run on, moving with a politician's ease onto firmer ground, where I can't be unseated by a difficult question or angered by a platitude. People aren't mind readers, so we have to signpost where we want the conversation to go. We can change the subject, keep things light, ask for support.

My son died, and it was a terrible time, but I'm mostly okay now. Did you hear about the hospital closure? Terrible news. I think there's a petition...

My son died, and I'm struggling today. It's good to take my mind off it—tell me something interesting.

My son died, and I could do with a friend. Bring the tissues.

———

When my father died, I found myself lost for words again. *My parents* were a linguistic entity it was impossible to separate, and this new language tripped me up many times. *Oh yes, my parents live there*, I'd say, and the mistake was a needle in my heart.

My mother lives there. Just my mother now.

I'd always known the power of words, but I was feeling them now in a new, visceral way.

There is a moment when you realize you have to now refer to your loved one in the past tense instead of the present. It feels like a betrayal, doesn't it? And more than that, it feels impossible, because they're still there, inside us, all around us.

I practiced an answer to the question *Where do your parents live?* until I didn't have to hesitate. Just as I directed exchanges about Alex, so I steered my conversations about my parents depending on how I felt or whether it really mattered that the other person knew my father had died. If you're thinking, *This all sounds terribly time-consuming*, I promise it isn't. It's an instinctive, fleeting decision—the way you know when it's safe to cross a road.

The questions that are difficult for me to answer may not be difficult for you. For you, perhaps it's *Do you have siblings?* or *Are your children coming for Christmas?* Maybe it's to do with a place, or a date: *Did you do anything nice for Father's Day?*

If there's a question you dread and wonder how to answer without breaking down, have a go at some practice answers. Take charge. Answer from the heart, or the head; answer honestly, or sidestep the question.

If your partner died, and the lead-in to Valentine's Day is making your heart hurt, have a dry run in your head, just in case someone asks if you'll be doing something nice. If they do, you can flip through your mental folder of well-rehearsed answers and slide out the one that feels right for that person, that moment. Your story is yours, and yours alone, and you can give away as much or as little as you want to.

Not a chance—load of commercial nonsense!

Or: *I haven't really thought about it.*

Or: *My wife died six months ago, and I'm dreading it.*

Your narrative. Your choice.

If you say something you think is stupid (it won't be), don't worry about it—it's your prerogative as a grieving person to mess up occasionally. If you say something that makes the other person uncomfortable, that's their problem, not yours. You won't be alone. There have been times when I've misjudged my tone so badly I've left acquaintances horrified by my apparent indifference. I've been so anxious to avoid sympathy—knowing it would break me—that I've plastered a grin on my face and followed *My son died* with a bellow of *But it's fine! Totally fine! Great, in fact! Hey, nice coat—where's it from?*

I never said I was an expert at this…

———

We are unpredictable, we mourners. Sometimes we want to talk; sometimes we long for silence. At times we seek distraction; other times we want to pick the scab of grief until it bleeds afresh. The important thing to remember is that we're the ones who get to decide. I've had media training several times, as a police officer and as an author, and the advice has always been identical: take charge of your narrative. We can't control what other people are going to say, but we have total autonomy over our own words.

Your choice.

Your conversation.

Your grief.

———

Over time, I've found I don't need the mental gymnastics as often. I know instinctively what to say, and how it will make me feel, and there aren't many questions that can derail me. It gets easier, I promise.

I still don't always give the same answers.

It depends on who I'm talking to, or how I'm feeling; on whether it's small talk at a publishing party or a chat over a cup of tea with a new friend. Mostly, when I'm asked how many children I have, I say three. Three is the number of plates at the table, sports uniforms in the wash, hugs at bedtime. Three is the correct answer.

But because this is you, and I know you'll understand, I'll give you the answer that feels more truthful.

How many children do I have?

Three in my home, four in my heart.

15

I promise you will be happy again

I was in my in-laws' sitting room, tea and cake on a series of small tables. Around us, my children were playing with their cousins, pulling out every train and car from the wicker toy box. Everyone—children and adults—was smiling, and I suddenly couldn't bear it. There was such a vast chasm between this lovely scene and the deep-rooted unhappiness I felt inside, and it was all I could do to stop myself from howling. I excused myself and went upstairs to splash water on my face and give myself a talking-to. I was so tired of feeling this way. I'd taken happiness for granted before Alex died, and now the very concept felt impossible.

No one I knew ever said, *Aren't you over that by now?* but I convinced myself they wanted to. Every article I read seemed to set an impossible target of "getting over" my grief, as though it were a teenage breakup from which I could bounce back in a matter of weeks, and here I was—years afterward—still fundamentally unhappy. The pressure to recover felt almost physical.

When someone we love dies, it infuses us with a sadness that alters us to our core. It is as though our DNA has been irrevocably altered, impacting our ability to achieve states that came so naturally before we were bereaved.

Of all those states, happiness always felt the furthest away to me. It's hard even to imagine it, the way it's impossible to remember the summer's heat wave when you're so cold you cannot feel your toes. Happiness is a place we visited a long time ago; a place to which we can't imagine returning, because it belonged to another lifetime entirely.

The facade of happiness returns long before happiness itself does. We laugh at jokes, order a round of drinks, share gossip from work, and blow out birthday candles, yet underneath it all is our grief. It can feel, for a long time, as though we're only *pretending* to be happy, and not only do I think that's okay, I think it can help us become *truly* happy. The more we smile, the more normal it begins to feel, even if we haven't smiled for a long time. Science backs this up: our brain can't tell the difference between a pretend smile and a real one; both trigger the release of chemicals that make us feel good.

Sometimes, if our facade is a good one, the people around

us forget that underneath we're still crumbling. Several years after Alex died, I had one of those days when grief rushed up on me like a freight train. You'll have had many such moments, I'm sure; triggered by nothing, yet impossible to stop.

In the midst of my despair, the doorbell rang, and I cleaned myself up as best I could, but you know what it's like—you can't hide the puffy, reddened eyes.

My friend stared at me aghast. "Oh my God, what's happened?"

I'd seen her just a few hours before, and most days that week. We'd been for drinks, roaring with laughter after one too many gins.

I told her what she already knew. "My son died."

"I…" She searched for a reason. She was wondering, perhaps, if today was a birthday, an anniversary.

"It's just one of those days." I smiled, minimizing her discomfort, as we often do.

"I always think how well you're doing," she said helplessly.

And I *was* doing well. *Am* doing well. But "doing well" doesn't mean we've gotten over our loss; it just means we're better at hiding our grief. Better at protecting ourselves. It means we've become skilled at acting, at steering conversations to avoid difficult subjects. It means we're careful about the places we visit and the things we do, because they can make us remember, and remembering hurts. It means we cry more on the inside than on the outside.

Over time, the gap between our pretend happiness and the real thing closes. We wrap our grief tighter inside us, and each year we build around it, until it's so well hidden even we can sometimes forget it's there. It becomes an old injury that once had you bedridden but which now simply gives you pain from time to time—when the weather's cold or you walk for too long.

———

The pursuit of happiness is a tough one, because it means different things to different people. For a long time, whenever I thought about happiness, it was in an abstract, objective way, as though I were analyzing an artifact no longer in use. I thought of Prince Charles in that infamous interview with Diana, and his devastating throwaway line: "Whatever love is." That's how I thought of happiness. *Whatever happiness is.* I was neither happy nor unhappy. I just *was*. Surviving, not thriving. Grief numbed my senses the way some drugs do, subduing my reactions and leaving me flat. I had so much to be happy about, yet everything felt sepia-toned, like an old photograph, faded by the years.

I think it's helpful to try and pin down what happiness means to you personally, what it is exactly that we're trying to achieve. *I want to feel happy* is broad and imprecise; *I want to enjoy walking along the river again* is much more specific. We can't have our walking companions back, but is there someone else we know who might keep us company? Could we borrow a dog to give us a different perspective on our surroundings? Sometimes the most stubborn obstacle to happiness is simply that we feel guilty even contemplating being happy. Remember: no one who loved you would ever want you to be *un*happy.

———

When someone dies, it skews our negativity bias, so we pay more attention to the bad things in our life. We can tip the scales back the other way by deliberately noting the positives and by intentionally saying or doing things that release positivity. When I wake up feeling unhappy—whether for an obvious reason or because of something I can't put my finger on—I make myself shower and put on proper clothes. I find a reason to walk into town instead of taking the dogs across the fields, because I know that what I need is a positive human interaction. I buy something small, pass the time of day with the cashier. I say, *Awful weather, isn't it?* to a woman waiting for the post office to open. I tell someone I love their umbrella, and stop a car from driving off with a freshly bought coffee on the roof. Small darts of dopamine, each one boosting my mood.

Happiness is not a destination. It's a constant state, a sliding scale across which we move from day to day and year to year. We can turn the dial ourselves; perhaps not all the way to the end, but in small, important ways. We can remind ourselves we have a purpose, by doing our job well or helping someone out. We can revisit hobbies that brought us joy when we were children or learn a new skill that has no association with our grief. We can practice self-care and feel contentment from a hot bath or nourishing food.

———

Life is short. You and I have learned that the hard way. It isn't surprising, then, that lots of us make big life changes in the wake of losing someone close. I would recommend a cautious approach to decisions (your experience might be different, but I wasn't capable of properly evaluating risk for some time after my son died), but death can bring a fresh perspective on the way we want to live our lives. After my father died, I couldn't settle at work. He'd been a National Health Service consultant, rarely taking holidays and working through evenings and weekends. He had grand plans for retirement—a trip on the Orient Express; the purchase of an unsuitable sports car—but cancer put an end to them all.

If Alex and my father hadn't died within a few years of each other, I suspect I might still be a police officer. Their deaths forced me to re-evaluate my priorities and work out what I really wanted out of life, and although quitting a secure job was terrifying, grief had made me brave. We've survived the unthinkable, haven't we?

We can do anything.

———

If you're reading this, I suspect you feel happiness is a long way off. It might even seem unattainable; the finishing line of a marathon you haven't trained for and that you began against your will. I understand. Finding joy after loss is a long and gradual process. The *if onlys* that follow us around (*if only they were here, if only they could see this*) take the edge off every moment we know should be wonderful. We can't will ourselves into happiness, but we can be open to it. We can notice the small spaces between the sadness, and allow those spaces to grow in their own time. We can remind ourselves—as many times as is necessary—that being happy is not a betrayal.

I have deliberately left this chapter until late in this book, because so much of what makes us happy is influenced by my earlier promises to you. Once you're sleeping properly, once the crying is under control, once you've learned to ride the waves, once the anger has passed, once you've found people who understand…

You'll be happy again. I promise.

———

I've taken the kids out for lunch. It strikes me—not for the first time—how lucky they are. How spoiled, I suppose, although I hope they never behave that way. When I was their age, meals out were a rare celebration: a few times a year, for special birthdays or a treat at the end of a fortnight in the caravan. My father—often distracted by work—would be for that brief period totally focused on us. Funny, interesting, irreverent. Conversations would be derailed by his tangents into the etymology of a particular word, noted down to look up when we got home, or by a joke he'd be unable to finish for laughing.

When the bill arrived, he would—without fail—do a comedy double take.

"How much?" he'd say, far too loudly. He would clutch his chest and loll his tongue, as though the tallied numbers had caused a seizure, and I'd sink into my seat, mortified beyond words.

"Don't!" I'd beg, too embarrassed to look around the restaurant to see who might be watching, thinking we had no money and were refusing to pay. The pantomime was agonizingly elaborate and seemingly endless.

Perhaps because I'm thinking of my father, I see a man

at another table who looks so much like him I catch my breath. The same thinning hair, the same creased pockets in his jacket. The same way of leaning back in his chair, holding court. But then he turns to attract the attention of a waiter, and the resemblance passes. I smile.

"What is it?" one of my children asks.

"Oh, nothing," I say. "I was just thinking of something nice." I glance at the bill and fall back in my seat, aghast. "*How* much?"

"Don't!" come the horrified cries.

But of course, I do.

16

I promise you'll be able to pay it forward

I was at work, trawling through the many emails into which I'd been copied, when I noticed one marked *Personal*. It was from a senior officer who was sharing in confidence that a member of their team had recently lost a child after a short and unexpected illness. *I wondered if you'd be happy to talk to her,* the email read. *I think it would help her to be in touch with someone who's come out the other side.*

I clicked *reply*, then left my cursor to blink in the empty reply box.

Happy was a poor choice of word, I reflected, almost objectively. No one is *happy* to talk about death. But was I open to it? Was I *willing*?

I swiveled my chair toward the opposite corner of my desk and began opening mail, buying myself time. Had I really "come out the other side"? I was still alive, which perhaps was enough of a qualification, but that seemed like a low bar. I was surviving, but I wasn't thriving.

As I tore open envelopes, I tried to pull apart the tangle of emotions I was experiencing. Part of me felt affronted by the suggestion that I was "better." I was four years or so into my grief, and I had indisputably made progress, but like all personal journeys, I took at least one step back for every two I took forward. My heart ached for this colleague's loss, but the brutal truth is that it ached more for my own.

I was scared, too. I was scared of what it would do to me if I heard her story (I could barely handle my own emotions; I wasn't ready to take on someone else's), and I was scared of making things worse for her. What if I broke down? This woman would be seeking confirmation that she could survive this; she would want me to promise things would get better. How would she feel when she was presented with a supposed role model who was patently not "better"?

I replied to the email. *Sorry, I'm not sure I'm the best person for this.* I added a list of books, websites, and support groups that might help instead. I pressed *send*.

My selfishness appalled me. I spent days in a sea of self-loathing, twice starting emails with *Actually, maybe I could…* then deleting them.

I couldn't; I just couldn't.

Grief is all-consuming. It is by its nature selfish, because it relates specifically to the way you feel—it is literally all about you and your personal response to the death of someone important to you. It's not only okay to feel that way (it's okay to feel any way you want), it's entirely normal. The person who died was your world, and when your world disintegrates, that becomes your focus. A castaway doesn't lose sleep over anyone's plight but their own.

Looking back, I can see I was almost territorial about bereavement: there was no room for anyone else's loss. I found it hard to separate the act of grieving from the object of grief itself, and so giving the stage to someone else felt like pushing my son into the shadows. The thought was unbearable. It was many years before I realized he wouldn't be standing in the shadows, only waiting in the wings.

I wonder if you recognize this territoriality in yourself, too. I know now that it is normal. I've moved past seeing it as something negative—a self-centeredness of which I was privately ashamed—and instead view it as something special and protective. While I was in this bubble, nothing else mattered. Nothing else could hurt me. It was just my son, my grief, and me.

It is, however, incompatible with paying it forward. Paying it forward means passing on your wisdom, your learnings. It means stepping aside to make space for someone else's feelings. It means putting yourself last.

Perhaps this feels a long way in the future. Maybe even impossible. I understand that. Maybe you even dread the prospect of being asked to help because you don't know what you'll say, how you'll react. All you know for certain is that you're not ready, and that's *fine*. More than fine. This chapter isn't here to make you anxious, but to prepare you. To prompt some thought and equip you with tools so that you know what might be on the horizon.

The transformation from supported to supporter is an organic one that occurs almost without you noticing. Over time, a friend's *Would it help to speak to someone I know who went through something similar?* becomes *Could you talk to someone I know who is grieving?* And perhaps this shift will happen organically, falling so perfectly in line with your own grief journey that you barely notice your role has changed, until one day you look up and realize you are holding a stranger's hand as they cry. But maybe it won't. Maybe your spotlight is still trained firmly on your own loss, and that's where it needs to stay.

It's okay to say no.

Grief is not your job. Your expertise doesn't come from studies and books, but from lived experience. That makes it the most valuable expertise there is, but sharing it comes at a cost. Helping other people means drawing on your personal reserves, on your memory, on your pain. It means opening yourself up to more hurt by creating the space and the empathy you know from experience the other person needs. Even if you never voice your own story, it will spool silently in your head and in your heart as they tell theirs. You'll relive it scene by scene, unable to switch off the movie you never asked to star in.

The supporter-supported relationship has a very different dynamic from that found within peer support groups, where the microphone passes equally around the room. As a supporter, you don't take the stage. You absorb the emotion of the person you're helping, without the catharsis of releasing your own, and that in itself can be exhausting. You assume the role of mentor. You're viewed as someone wise, someone further down the path than the person you're supporting, with advice and guidance at your fingertips.

This journey from *supported* to *supporter* is not a linear one. There are times when I willingly put myself forward as a supporter, when I listen to someone's story with no compulsion to share my own. In these cases, my son's death becomes an abstract concept, something that exists in the present moment only to add credibility to the coping strategies I gently suggest. *It might not work for you, but I found it helped to keep a journal, to call a friend, to keep myself busy.*

There are other times when I recognize I am not the person they need. That in spite of what they see—a woman eighteen years on from her son's death, a woman no longer crippled with pain—something has moved my grief dangerously close to the surface, and I cannot let it break through.

Finally, there are times when I get it wrong. When I say that *yes, of course I'd be happy to help*, and then I meet with the person with whom I've been paired, and I realize with a lurch that I've made a terrible mistake. That their pain is too raw, or too similar to mine, or simply too *much*, and I feel a torrent of grief inside me. Tears spring to my eyes, and I tell them how sorry I am for their loss, when really it's mine I'm crying for.

It can be tough to be cast in the role of bereavement supporter, however removed you are from your own loss, and I think that pulling away is sometimes the smart thing to do—for both parties. If you're not in the right place to offer support, the support you give will not be what's needed. Imagine a therapist who interrupted a counseling session to dry his own tears, a massage therapist too sore to pummel at your knotted back. There are always other people who can help.

If offering support in this way is not something you can do (the reasons don't matter—you never have to justify it, not to me, not to anyone), there are other ways to pay it forward if you would like to. You might find you're able to write about your experiences online, or for a newsletter produced by a hospice, and that your words will provide much-needed solace.

Perhaps you might share a link or a phone number for a bereavement service with your friends, ensuring more people know about a service they might one day need. Maybe you'll give feedback to the service providers who dealt with your loved one in their final days, so they can understand what's working and what isn't, and offer even better care in the future. Perhaps you'll give a copy of this book to a friend or to the local library, so more people can come across it.

Paying it forward is about more than offering a physical shoulder to cry on. It's about starting conversations and making space for other people's stories. It's about educating and informing, trying to make someone else's life a tiny bit better. It's about allowing something good to come out of something so terrible.

——

I have now traveled many miles since my son's death. Sometimes I can listen to a story of loss without holding up my own for comparison—without even thinking of how it was for me.

Sometimes.

On other occasions, I pick up the scent of sadness, and my heart squeezes so tight I don't trust myself to speak. I fight to change the subject, to move us onto safer ground as protection for us both, because I am out of my depth,. And if they cling to me, we'll both drown.

Ever since my first novel was published, I have been fortunate enough to be sent copies of upcoming books for possible endorsements. I've always been very open about my experiences of grief, and when these books explore loss—particularly the loss of a child—the editor will often include a note. *I hope this beautiful portrayal of grief speaks to you*, it might say, or *I think you will relate to this one.*

Sometimes (and I am so very grateful for these) the note simply says, *Only read if you're able to.*

I am often unable. There are times when I can't even have the book on my shelf; other times when I start reading, I have to close the pages because I could have written the words myself, because I know they will undo me. I stop not because the books are bad, but because they're too good, because it's as though my emotions have been torn from me and placed on the page, and it's too much for me to take.

I feel guilty because I know that "paying it forward" as an author means to lift up other writers, and who better to endorse a book on grief than someone who can say, hand on aching heart, that every word is true?

I'm a writer. I can write about grief more easily than I can read about it; I can write about it more easily than I can speak about it. This book is my way of paying it forward, of reaching people who want support. There have been times in the writing of it that I have had to stop and catch my breath, times when I've had to close the file and walk away, often for weeks at a time.

When we offer support, it's okay for it to be on our terms. It's okay for us to qualify that support by controlling the *when*, the *who*, the *how much*.

Only read if you're able to.

Say yes to supporting a bereaved person if you're able to.

Listen to their story if you're able to.

Pay it forward if you're ready. Make your peace with it if you're not.

———

It's been more than three years since I first made my "promises for grief." I log on to my Twitter account and check my messages, as I do most days. I delete the unwanted ones and skim the rest, because although they all merit a response, some messages need answering faster than others.

I lost my dad in February...

My sister took her own life...

I miss my wife so much I can't bear it...

They write because the promises spoke to them. Because my words gave them a glimmer of hope, and because it is human nature to reach out when we feel a connection. Nowadays I receive only a handful of messages each week, but in the first few months after I posted the promises, there were thousands. My inbox became a living thing, constantly changing shape as new messages pushed down the ones before. I felt scared. What could I say to these people when they asked for advice? I wasn't a psychotherapist or a grief counselor. I felt like a fraud.

But they didn't want advice. They wanted to tell me their stories and thank me for offering hope. They wanted to tell me who they'd sent the promises to, and why my words had come at exactly the right time. They wanted to say thank you.

In my inbox today is a message from someone with whom I have corresponded before. I scroll up to remind myself of the context and let out a breath as I feel her heartache again. This first message had come soon after I'd posted the promises—several years after her teenage son had been killed in an accident—when she'd been mired in despair.

It's a living hell, she'd written. *Every day, I want to die too.*

I'm so sorry, I'd replied. Those words always feel inadequate, don't they? But when we say it and mean it, they're really the only words we need to say. *Sorry for your loss, for what you're going through, for the hell you're enduring. So very, very sorry this happened to you.* It is a small thing to do, to offer some words as comfort, but paying it forward doesn't have to be extravagant. Sometimes it's the small things we do that make the biggest difference.

Today's message is longer than her first.

I saved your promises, she said. *I read them when I felt like I couldn't do this. I came across them again today, and they made me realize how far I've come. It's still awful, but I'm doing okay.*

I let out a breath. I have heard thousands of stories of grief, but rarely do I learn how the story has continued. I feel privileged to have been part of this woman's journey, and grateful to her for writing back. I think of the woman who came to my door with the daffodils, and I think that, maybe, I've paid it forward.

17

I promise you won't forget

After Alex died, I lost my memory. It didn't disappear entirely, but it became slippery and unreliable, like a bad friend who turns up late, or not at all. I forgot birthdays and appointments; I forgot the names of people I'd known for years. Events in my recent past felt hazy, as though I were recalling stories I'd heard secondhand instead of experiencing them myself.

One day, I stood in the bathroom, racking my brains to remember why I was there. I stared at the stranger in the mirror, with her hollow cheeks and shadowed eyes, running through the reasons people visited bathrooms. I didn't need the toilet or a tissue. I was already dressed, so I couldn't have come in for a shower. I opened drawers, searching for a prompt, before realizing I was holding my toothbrush. Somewhere between picking it up and putting toothpaste on it, I'd forgotten what I was doing.

I found this loss of control terrifying. I'd been put in charge of three small children, yet I could barely look after myself. A few days later, parked in the driveway of our house, I stared at the dashboard of the car as though I'd never driven before, until muscle memory kicked in and I remembered how to turn on the ignition.

Grief brain is, as the young people say, *a thing*. It is as much a phenomenon as the baby brain given as a self-deprecating explanation by many mothers in the immediate aftermath of a new arrival. The adjective is interchangeable. Divorce brain, exam-nerves brain, first-love brain: preoccupations and obsessions that consume us so completely there is no room for anything else. Nothing else is important.

But while we can make jokes about forgetting your head if it wasn't screwed on, or discovering you've put your keys in the fridge instead of in the drawer, it is terrifying to feel as though you're losing your mind. I'd put jacket potatoes in the oven, then forget to take them out; realize in the frozen food aisle that I was still wearing my slippers. Baby brain and first-love brain pass quickly (the baby becomes a toddler, the heady infatuation of new love fades), but with grief, we're in it for the long haul. I was terrified my unreliable memory would be permanent.

If you're struggling with forgetfulness, you'll be relieved to hear it was not. I often find that the more we try not to think about something, the more it forces its way into our mind, and in that period of time, I was trying very hard not to think about grief. I was pushing it as far down inside me as I could, certain it would break me if I let it rise to the surface. But grief is far stronger than us, and it was still such early days for me.

I began, tentatively, to let a little of my grief out. To assess myself in the morning and plan my day according to how I felt, not what I thought I should be doing. Acknowledging my grief seemed to make it quieter, like an excitable dog that settles down once everyone has said hello. Before long, I had more space in my head again and my memory began to stabilize.

This is not rocket science—who among us doesn't become more forgetful and distracted when something big is happening in our lives?—but I'm sharing it here because, like me, you might not recognize what's happening at the time. It might feel scary, and as though you'll always feel this way, so I hope it helps to see that it's normal and transient, like so many of the symptoms of grief.

———

If beginning to unpick my grief helped my short-term memory to settle, it seemed to have the opposite effect on how I remembered the past. As I recovered, I found I could hardly recall the first time I held my son or how it felt to change his onesie. Our time together was spent in a single room. There were no extravagant trips of a lifetime or family gatherings, only quiet moments of hope and despair. On the day he died, I changed his clothes and washed his hair, read him stories and sang lullabies, trying to squeeze a lifetime of memories into those final few hours. The experience was heartbreakingly visceral; every sense activated, every nerve ending filled with love and grief. Now, I could no longer remember the weight of him in my arms, the smell of his head. I couldn't recall the exact shade of his hair, or how it felt to have his fingers curl around mine. Five weeks was not enough time to make memories that would last.

When my father died, I sat down to write his eulogy, only to find my memory was letting me down once again. There was so much I'd forgotten. I remembered my father in an abstract way, as though I were describing him to someone else, instead of feeling it inside. The more I tried to capture the essence of him, the more he slipped away, until I was unclear whether I was thinking of him or a memory of him, like an anecdote told so many times you're no longer sure where it originated. It seemed thirty-five years wasn't enough time, either.

How much time did *you* have?

Two years? Thirty? Fifty?

It wasn't enough, was it? How could it be? It's never enough. Not enough to build the memories we want or to burn them so fiercely on our hearts that we will never forget them.

And yet I promise you will not forget. Not really.

———

I am constantly fascinated by my children's memories, by the way milestone events can pass without a shadow, yet the tiniest of occasions can be etched on their minds.

"We've been here before!" one of mine piped up once—they were perhaps four or five years old—as we pulled into the nondescript car park of a supermarket I didn't recall ever having visited. "I was wearing trousers with pockets!" My children remember obscure things: dried apricots eaten on an airplane at eighteen months old. Clowns they met at Legoland when all three were still in diapers. The middle name of a classmate they last saw ten years ago.

But when I ask them about their grandfather, confusion creeps across their faces. "Did he have white hair?" one asks, full of doubt. I smile and nod, but I'm cracking inside, realizing my children are growing up without the influence of the cleverest, kindest man I have known. So much of my grief for my father isn't about my own relationship with him at all, but about the fact that he didn't get to see my children as young adults.

"We used to sit on his lap to have a story," another says.

I seize on this apparent recollection. "You did! He read you lots of stories!"

The others chip in, elaborating on the memory, but I see their eyes flick across the kitchen to where a handful of photos are pinned to a board. In one, my father sits beneath a pile of children, reading *The Gruffalo* aloud. I feel a balloon expanding in my chest, and I think I might burst. They're describing a picture. They don't remember, not really.

"He showed me how to wind the grandfather clock," my eldest says suddenly. He tells us how he was allowed to open the cabinet, how the hundred-year-old key was stiff in his little hand. How Grandad lifted him up to turn the hands on the clock face, and how the chimes rang out every time they passed twelve. He tells it with such conviction that the balloon in my chest softens, in such detail that I can see it, too. This memory wasn't mine, but it is now.

There's a reason why many people find a sense of peace in funerals and memorial services. Yes, they provide a form of closure, but more than that, they give us an opportunity to remember. Tributes from old friends allow us an insight into who people were before we met them, or remind us of stories we thought we'd forgotten. Standing in a church hall eating curled-up sandwiches is a chance to share our memories and deepen our understanding of our loved ones, but we don't need to confine these conversations to wakes. If you feel your memories of someone are becoming evasive—and if you feel strong enough to do so—try talking to someone else who knew them. Memories are fickle beasts, as easily woken up as they are rendered dormant, and shared conversations can revive moments you might have thought were lost. Talking about the people we've loved and lost can help us keep them alive in our collective memories.

———

Sometimes, talking is too much. We want to keep our grief private, or we can't find the words to share it, or there is no one who knew our loved one well enough. There are other ways to remember. You can take out their clothes, or look at photographs. Read a book they loved and run your finger over the folds in the corner. Cook from old recipe cards, written out in careful script, or from annotations in the margins of a well-worn cookbook. *Not a huge success—try with three eggs?* Not only do these tangible items serve as memory prompts, they also strengthen our connections to those no longer with us.

My first novel is dedicated to my son. When it was published, I saw it in train stations and airports across the country, in supermarkets and huge chain stores and quaint little bookshops in market squares. When it sold a million copies, I took a moment to imagine that many people picking it up, assessing the cover, creasing the spine. I imagined them reading the words on that very first page.

For Alex.

My boy, remembered a million times and counting.

This is what we do. We plant trees and carve names into stone. We fix plaques to benches. We run races with their names blazoned across our chests. We write books for them. This is how we honor them, how we tell strangers about them. This is how we remember them.

———

When I want to remember my son—really remember him—I open the box in which I keep his belongings. I touch the inked handprint, and the impossibly small footprint. I read the headlines on the newspaper from the day he was born. The physical objects prompt a wave of memories I'm ready for. I remember his miniature fingernails, translucent pink and so sharp he cut himself. I remember his jerk of surprise as I tickled the soles of his feet; remember brushing his hair and wondering if the red (my own contribution to his genes) would stay. I remember the conversations with other parents on the ward; the kindness of the nurses. The overwhelming joy I felt as I was wheeled down to neonatal intensive care unit to meet my sons; the magic of the moment our eyes first met. I remember it all. I haven't forgotten.

———

I'm still capable of walking into a room and immediately forgetting why I'm there, but I'm reliably informed I have that in common with a great many people my age. I have regained the clarity of thought I once had, the sharpness I took for granted before I was bereaved. I've come to realize that forgetting is part of the process of grieving. Forgetting how it felt to be clutched by pain, to feel the world crashing around your feet. Forgetting the awfulness of those early days.

Like the tide sweeping across a pebbled beach, time softens the hard edges of our memories, and sometimes it feels as though we're losing the smooth along with the rough. But we have only to close our eyes and walk slowly back through the moments that mattered. They're all there, carefully filed away. We haven't forgotten. Not really.

18

I promise it won't always hurt like this

I know: I've already made this promise. But I want this to be the one you see if you're a person who looks at the end of a book first. I want it to stick in your mind if you've now read it twice, or if you're reading it last, because this promise is the most important one. It's also the hardest to believe. The pain of early bereavement is so intense, it's impossible to imagine it ever receding. It will. Trust me.

I imagine grief plotted on a chart, like the London Stock Exchange or the milestones of a serial dieter. Time marching along the bottom: our survival charted first in hours, then weeks and months, then years. Along the side, markers of emotional wellbeing: happy, stable, broken. A thick black line scores our halting progress through grief, beginning off the scale in the abyss of new loss—the raw, choking pain impossible to describe to those who haven't felt it.

If you could look into the future, you would see the line on your graph rising slowly but steadily. It will be interrupted, at times, by sharp downward dives, but it will rise again, the curve continuing. Upward, ever upward.

There was a time, a few years after Alex died, when I realized my recovery had slowed. Time continued to tick away, but the line that had once headed steadfastly toward the sky now pointed only eastward. Neither north nor south. It remained that way for two, maybe three years. *This is as good as it gets*, I wrote in my diary. Neither happy nor sad, neither better nor worse. I remember the clutch of despair as I realized I would forever feel this way, my grief solid and heavy inside me. This was as good as I was ever going to feel.

I was wrong.

I don't know why my recovery slowed when it did, for the time that it did, but it must have been what my head and heart needed back then. Because in its own sweet time, that thick black line started climbing again.

———

This year, my son would have turned eighteen. He'd be driving a car, visiting universities, planning a gap year of travel and adventures. He might have been passionate about sport, or music, or theater, have become obsessed with space, or trees, or computers. He and his twin brother might have been inseparable.

It's painful to think of what might have been, and I try to remember how pointless it is—no one knows what any of us might have achieved had we not taken the paths we did. I might have stayed in the police and become a senior officer, but I became a writer instead. I might have brought four children safely back from hospital, but I only came home with three. Life is full of forks in the road, each one taking us in a different direction. Sometimes we have the luxury of deciding which path to take, of turning back and trying another route if we don't like the first. Other times we have no choice but to continue walking, making the best of the journey.

You and I didn't choose this path we're on. We didn't want to meet here in this club no one ever asks to join. Yet here we are, walking if not side by side then in similar directions, searching for the people we were before grief swallowed us whole.

It's hard not to imagine what my son would be doing now. Hard to see his twin brother head off to school each morning and not wonder which subjects Alex would have chosen. Every year that passes, every milestone missed, is a splinter to the heart.

But these moments are milestones for us, too. They're

medals, fought for and to be worn with pride. They're proof that we're still standing, that we've kept our head above water for another year. The journey through grief is not an easy one. It is stepping stones across a river, some easier to navigate than others. Sometimes we slip and fall into the water, and it would be easy to lie there, drowning in grief, but we didn't do that. *You* didn't do that. You got up.

You found your footing again and you kept going. You read this book.

Every time we fall, it becomes a little easier to get back up. The morphine for grief is time. Time does not in itself heal, but it shows us we can keep going. It softens the edges of our pain and puts distance between us and our loss so we can see it more clearly. It shows us life is worth living, even without our loved ones in it.

———

Eighteen years ago, I had to remind myself to breathe. Every day, I made myself get up, made myself put one foot in front of the other, until one day I didn't have to remember. I was simply walking. Breathing, standing, walking. Surviving, not thriving—but surviving nonetheless.

As time passed, I grew around my grief, the way a tree grows around iron railings.

I began to live again.

I began to thrive.

I am not "better." I'm in recovery, and there will always be days when I slip backward. I suspect I'll always change the television channel when they show babies in intensive care, that I'll always feel reflective when I see a set of twins. I'll always miss my son. I'll always cry for him. I'll always wish life had dealt us a different hand. But I know, too, that I'll always smile at daffodils, grateful for the woman who came to my door with a promise I never thought would come true. I am more than my grief now, and you will be, too.

If you are overwhelmed by the mere act of existing, I promise—with all my heart—it will get better. Just get through today. If that's too much, get through the next hour, the next minute, a single second. One step at a time, one breath at a time.

I promise you, as I walk side by side with you in your grief, that it will get better.

It will not always hurt like this.

A few practical things that have helped me:

Books

Exercise

Being in nature

Taking a shower

Writing down how I feel

Making lists

Helping other people

Cold-water swimming

Comfort food

Wearing cozy clothes

Repeats of favorite TV shows

Being with animals

Turning off the internet

Allowing myself to grieve

Resources

I have found the following books helpful:

Non-fiction
The Five People You Meet in Heaven, Mitch Albom
The Madness of Grief, the Reverend Richard Coles
The Year of Magical Thinking, Joan Didion
Reasons to Stay Alive, Matt Haig
A Manual for Heartache, Cathy Rentzenbrink
Grief Works, Julia Samuel

Fiction
The Phone Box at the Edge of the World, Laura Imai Messina
Hamnet, Maggie O'Farrell
Grief is the Thing with Feathers, Max Porter
The Trick to Time, Kit de Waal

Acknowledgments

I never planned to write this book, and I wouldn't have done so if it hadn't been for the extraordinary response to the tweets I posted on Alex's anniversary. For that reason, the most important thanks must go to the thousands of people who shared with me their own stories of grief and recovery. I tried so hard to reply to everyone, but the messages came in as fast as I answered them. If you wrote to me, please know that I read your words and was moved by them, and that you are the inspiration behind this book. In writing it, I have worked through another layer of my grief, and for that, too, I am grateful. Thank you.

I worried that writing a book on grief was self-indulgent, that it was arrogant of me to assume I had anything new to say. I'm so grateful to my agents, Emily Harris and Sheila Crowley, who offered unfailing support from the moment I tentatively mentioned the project, and who found a home for it with the wonderful team at Sphere. Emily Barrett brought her own experiences of grief to these pages, guiding me through the editorial process with extraordinary care and insight. It has been a privilege to work with her.

There are so many friends, old and new, who have supported me through my grief and in the writing of this book. There isn't space to list you all, and that in itself is a wonderful thing to acknowledge. Thank you for being there for me.

Finally, my thanks to my family. This has been a difficult book to write, but writing it surrounded by love made the world of difference. I am so lucky to have you.

About the Author

©Jenny Aston

Clare Mackintosh is a former police officer and a multi-award-winning author. Translated into forty languages, her books have sold more than two million copies worldwide and have been *New York Times* and international bestsellers. Mackintosh has spoken on television and radio about the death of her son and the themes of grief and healing, which consequently appear in her novels. She lives in North Wales with her family and can be found at claremackintosh.com, or on Instagram and Facebook at @ClareMackWrites